Scott Foresman

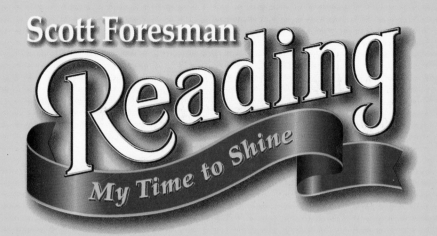

My Time to Shine

Ties Through Time

All Aboard!

Just Imagine!

Scott
Foresman

About the Cover Artist

Where John Sandford lives in Michigan, there are lots of small animals such as squirrels and chipmunks, but when he is painting an animal, he thinks about a person he knows. He says that thinking of a particular person as he works gives his animals personality.

ISBN 0-328-03934-9

1 2 3 4 5 6 7 8 9 10 V063 10 09 08 07 06 05 04 03 02

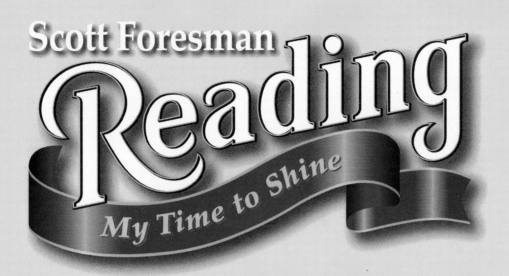

Scott Foresman Reading
My Time to Shine

Program Authors

Peter Afflerbach

James Beers

Camille Blachowicz

Candy Dawson Boyd

Wendy Cheyney

Deborah Diffily

Dolores Gaunty-Porter

Connie Juel

Donald Leu

Jeanne Paratore

Sam Sebesta

Karen Kring Wixson

Editorial Offices: Glenview, Illinois • Parsippany, New Jersey • New York, New York
Sales Offices: Parsippany, New Jersey • Duluth, Georgia • Glenview, Illinois
Coppell, Texas • Ontario, California

Contents

Ties Through Time

4

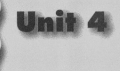

Unit 4

Contents

Unit 5

Contents

8

Unit 6

9

Ties Through Time

What things do
we do together
in the same
special way?

Hear the Cheers
by Diane Hoyt-Goldsmith

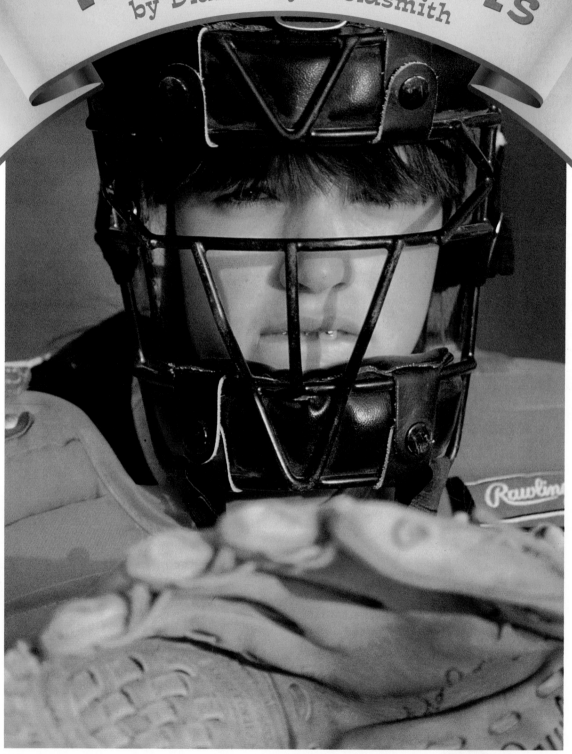

The batter waits for the pitch in a baseball game.

What can you play with a ball and a bat? You can play baseball. When the bat hits the ball, the fans cheer loudly. The ball sails clear out of the park. It's a home run!

There are nine players on the team. The only gear the batter needs is a helmet to cover the head and ears. The best time each year is when baseball teams compete in the World Series. Clearly, baseball is still one of our favorite sports.

Players race for the puck in a hockey game.

What can you play with a stick and a puck? You can play hockey. Players skate quickly and smoothly over the ice. The goalie stands near the net. Hockey players need to put on lots of gear. The game is rough, but the players have no fear. They pass and steer the puck with their sticks. They shoot the puck into the net. Score! The crowd cheers.

In the 1850s, lacrosse was a favorite game of the Sioux.

What game can you play with a ball and a stick? You can play lacrosse. Native Americans played lacrosse hundreds of years ago, and it is still popular.

For them it was more than a game. It helped them to be better deer hunters. It was also a way to solve problems peacefully. The team that won the game also won the argument. Native Americans had a good idea when they thought up the game of lacrosse.

Members of the Onondaga Nation, New York, play lacrosse today.

In lacrosse, players cannot touch the ball with their hands. They easily throw and catch the ball with the net on their sticks. When the ball goes into the goal, a point is scored. Then you can hear the cheers.

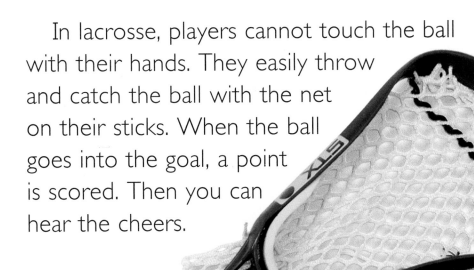

The Great Ball Game

A Muskogee Story

retold by
Joseph Bruchac

illustrated by
Susan L. Roth

Long ago the Birds and Animals had a great
argument.

"We who have wings are better than you," said
the Birds.

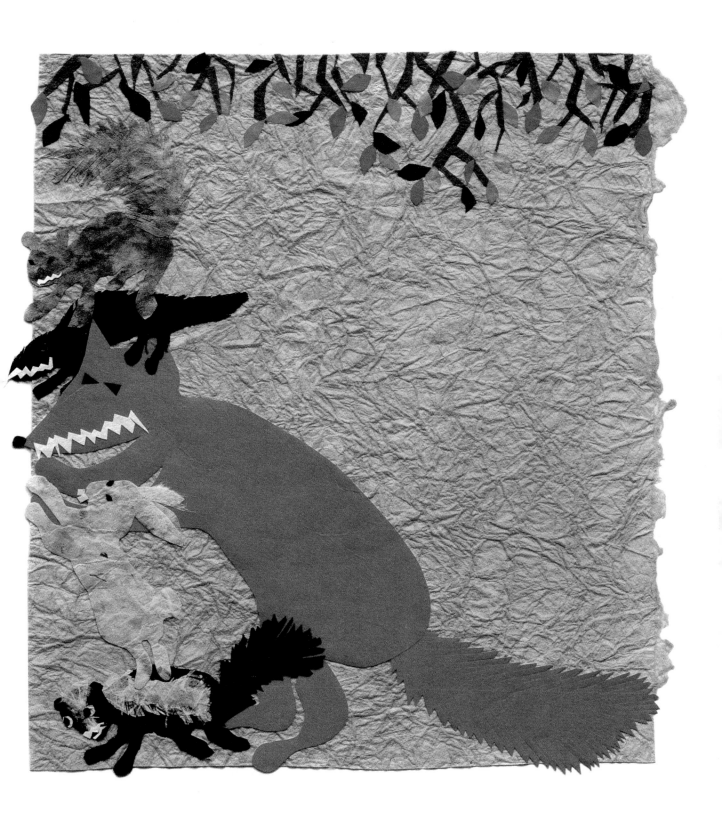

"That is not so," the Animals replied. "We who have teeth are better."

The two sides argued back and forth. Their quarrel went on and on, until it seemed they would go to war because of it.

Then Crane, the leader of the Birds, and Bear, the leader of the Animals, had an idea.

"Let us have a ball game," Crane said. "The first side to score a goal will win the argument."

"This idea is good," said Bear. "The side that loses will have to accept the penalty given by the other side."

So they walked and flew to a field, and there they divided up into two teams.

On one side
went all those
who had wings.
They were the
Birds.

On the other
side went those
with teeth. They
were the Animals.

But when the teams were formed, one creature was left out: Bat. He had wings *and* teeth! He flew back and forth between the two sides.

First he went
to the Animals. "I have
teeth," he said. "I must
be on your side."

But Bear shook his head. "It would not be fair,"
he said. "You have wings. You must be a Bird."

So Bat flew to the other side. "Take me," he said to the Birds, "for you see I have wings."

But the Birds laughed at him. "You are too little to help us. We don't want you," they jeered.

Then Bat went back to the Animals. "Please let me join your team," he begged them. "The Birds laughed at me and would not accept me."

So Bear took pity on the little bat. "You are not very big," said Bear, "but sometimes even the small ones can help. We will accept you as an Animal, but you must hold back and let the bigger Animals play first."

Two poles were set up as the goalposts at each end of the field. Then the game began.

Each team played hard. On the Animals' side Fox and Deer were swift runners, and Bear cleared the way for them as they played. Crane and Hawk, though, were even swifter, and they stole the ball each time before the Animals could reach their goal.

Soon it became clear that the Birds had the advantage. Whenever they got the ball, they would fly up into the air and the Animals could not reach them. The Animals guarded their goal well, but they grew tired as the sun began to set.

Just as the sun sank below the horizon, Crane took the ball and flew toward the poles. Bear tried to stop him, but stumbled in the dim light and fell. It seemed as if the Birds would surely win.

Suddenly a small dark shape flew onto the field and stole the ball from Crane just as he was about to reach the poles. It was Bat. He darted from side to side across the field, for he did not need light to find his way. None of the Birds could catch him or block him.

Holding the ball, Bat flew right between the poles at the other end! The Animals had won!

This is how Bat came to be accepted as an Animal. He was allowed to set the penalty for the Birds.

"You Birds," Bat said, "must leave this land for half of each year."

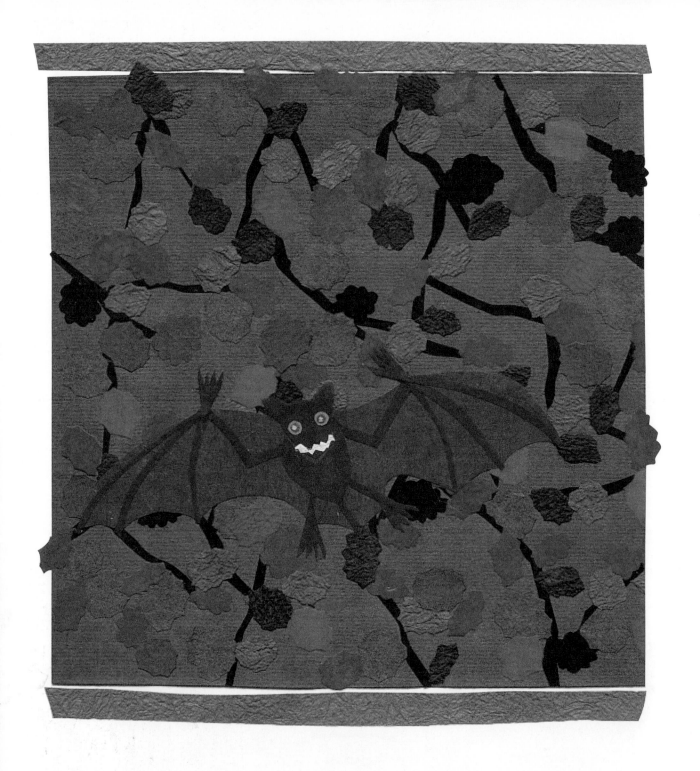

So it is that the Birds fly south each winter.
And every day at dusk Bat still comes flying to see
if the Animals need him to play ball.

About the Author
Joseph Bruchac

Joseph Bruchac enjoyed the Native American stories he learned as a child. He first told them to his sons. Then he began retelling them in books and performing them for others. Today he is a performing storyteller. Mr. Bruchac's Abenaki Indian name is Sozap.

About the Illustrator
Susan L. Roth

Susan L. Roth uses torn and cut paper to create her work. In *The Great Ball Game,* she used papers from around the world to make her pictures. Ms. Roth has also written children's books.

Reader Response

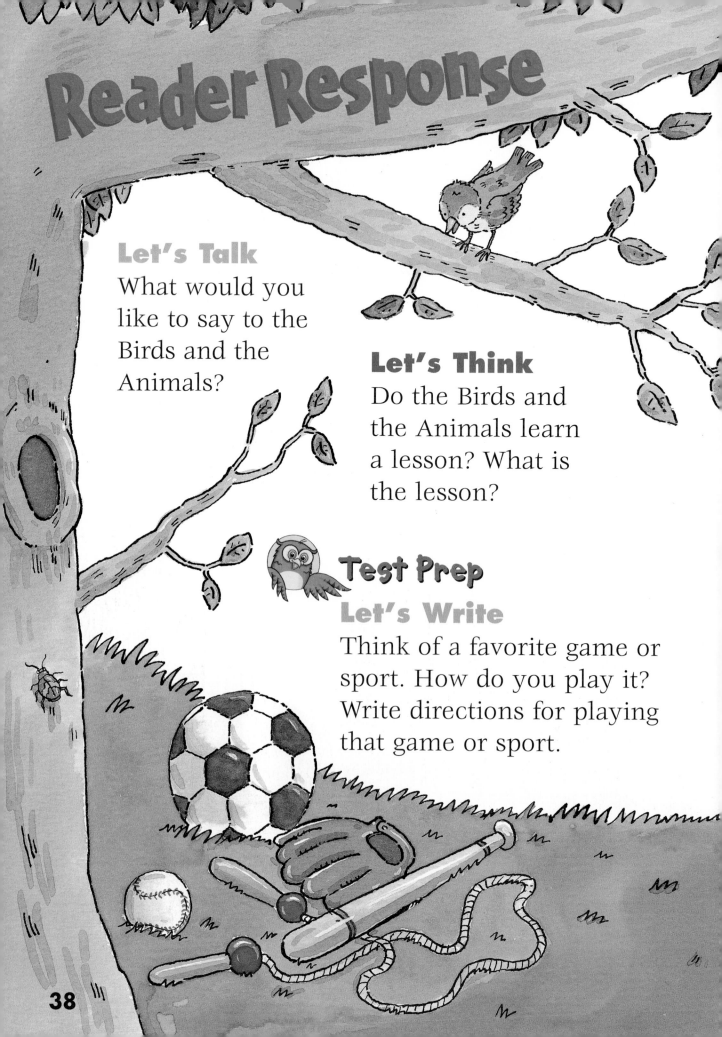

Let's Talk
What would you like to say to the Birds and the Animals?

Let's Think
Do the Birds and the Animals learn a lesson? What is the lesson?

Test Prep
Let's Write
Think of a favorite game or sport. How do you play it? Write directions for playing that game or sport.

Act It Out

Pretend that Bat joined the Birds' team instead of the Animals' team. Act out a new ending.

1. Work in a group. Think of one way that Bat could help the Birds.
2. Make up a new ending for the story. Tell what Bat does to help the Birds.
3. Choose parts and practice acting out the new ending.
4. Act out the new ending for your classmates.

Language Arts

Adjectives

An **adjective** describes a noun. An adjective may tell how many, what size, or what shape.

Ten animals are on the playground.

Kick the **round** ball.

The **little** rabbit jumps rope.

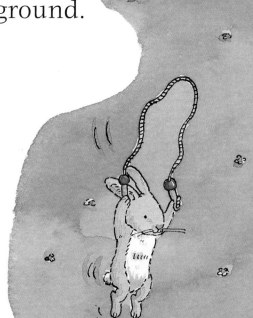

adjective	noun
Ten	animals
round	ball
little	rabbit

Talk

Talk about the picture. Describe what you see. Use words that describe how many, what size, and what shape.

40

Write

Write the sentences. Circle the adjectives.

1. Who throws a big ball in the round hoop?
2. The little bear kicks the ball.
3. The animals use two balls.

Write sentences about the playground at your school. Use adjectives that tell how many, what size, or what shape.

Birthday Joy

by Anne Sibley O'Brien

When you have your birthday, is there a wonderful cake with candles? Do your friends join in to sing "Happy Birthday" to you? Do you get toys?

All over the world, boys and girls have different ways of having a joyful birthday. Has anyone ever told you about this?

In Germany, the birthday girl or boy has a beautiful birthday candle. The mother or father lights this important candle to point out the child's age. On each birthday, the candle burns down to the next number.

In Mexico, the birthday boy or girl might get a piñata. The father takes his child to the market to look about at all the different piñatas. The child might choose a colorful bird, a beautiful horse, or a dog with pointed ears. It is hard to make a choice!

Later, friends join the birthday child for a wonderful party. Each boy and girl tries to break the piñata. When it cracks, candy and toys spill about for everyone to enjoy!

In Israel, the birthday girl or boy gets a beautiful crown of flowers. The mother places the royal crown on her child's head. The child looks very important!

Then the birthday girl or boy sits in a special chair. The father is careful to raise the chair once for each year. Friends make noise and dance about as the chair goes up and down.

Now you have been told! All over the world, boys and girls enjoy their birthdays in many different ways.

The Best Older Sister

by Sook Nyul Choi
illustrated by Yoshi Miyake

1. No Time for Sunhi

Sunhi dragged her feet as she walked
home from school. Her grandmother,
Halmoni, had always waited for Sunhi
outside the schoolyard with a delicious
snack. Together they would walk home.
Sunhi would tell Halmoni all about her day
at school.

But everything changed for Sunhi
when her little brother, Kiju, was born.

Halmoni no longer had time to play with Sunhi. Now Halmoni was busy taking care of Kiju all day while Sunhi's mother and father were at work.

Halmoni fed him, bathed him, and changed his diapers. That little baby made such a mess and needed so much attention.

When Sunhi came home, she saw Halmoni sitting on the sofa, bouncing Kiju on her knee.

Halmoni was waving Sunhi's little brown teddy bear in front of Kiju. He smiled and drooled with delight.

Mrs. Lee and Mrs. Stone, their neighbors, were visiting. They were making silly noises as they admired the baby.

They hardly noticed Sunhi.

"Oh, hello, Sunhi," said Mrs. Lee, looking up finally. "We just stopped by to see Kiju.

"How adorable your little brother is! I can hardly believe he will be a year old next week."

"Halmoni told us that it is a Korean custom to have a big party on a baby's first birthday," said Mrs. Stone. "You must be so excited."

Sunhi managed a polite smile.

"It is so wonderful to have a boy in the family," said Mrs. Lee.

Sunhi was tired of all the fuss everyone made over this baby. She did not think he was so interesting. She wished one of these visitors would adopt him and take him away.

"Can I have my bear back? That is still mine, isn't it?"

Sunhi snatched it and ran to her room.

Everything was different with Kiju around. Even her room was not her own anymore. It was full of baby diapers and baby toys. It smelled like baby powder.

"How happy you must be to have a little brother!" everyone said to Sunhi.

"Isn't it wonderful to be a big sister now?" they asked.

But it did not seem so wonderful to Sunhi. Now her parents had even less time to talk to her and play with her in the evenings.

Most of all, Sunhi missed spending time with Halmoni. When Halmoni wasn't with Kiju, she was busy doing things for him.

Just yesterday Sunhi had caught Halmoni sewing secretly in her room. Sunhi saw the beautiful blue silk.

She knew that Halmoni must be making something for Kiju to wear on his birthday.

"What is so special about this little baby, anyway?" Sunhi wondered. "Why is it so important to have a boy? Wasn't I good enough?" Sunhi sobbed.

2. A Surprise for Sunhi

There was a gentle knock on the door.
Halmoni entered. She quietly sat beside Sunhi.

Halmoni wiped Sunhi's tears and stroked
her hair.

Halmoni said, "I have a surprise for you. I was going to save it until next week. But I think I will give it to you now."

"What is it, Halmoni?" Sunhi said. She swallowed her tears and brushed away Halmoni's hand.

"It is in your parents' room. Three big presents," said Halmoni.

"What? Those are all Kiju's!" said Sunhi.

Halmoni carried the three big boxes into Sunhi's room. "Come on, Sunhi. Sit up. Open this one first," she said.

In the box was a royal blue silk Korean
dress. It had rainbow-colored sleeves and
butterflies embroidered on the front. Sunhi
loved it.

"This is for you to wear on Kiju's birthday,"
said Halmoni. "I was afraid you saw it last
night when you came to say good night.

"These other two are for your best friends,
Jenny and Robin. Open them and see if you
think they will like them."

Jenny's was peach-colored with white rosebuds embroidered on the front. Robin's was yellow with tiny blue birds embroidered on the sleeves. Sunhi knew that her friends would love these.

"Halmoni, these are so pretty. It must have taken you a very long time to make them!" said Sunhi.

"Well, luckily Kiju is a good baby. He sleeps a lot. I am sorry I haven't taken you to school and picked you up. I have missed that.

"You are special to me. It is just that babies are so helpless and need a lot of care. Just like when you were a baby," said Halmoni.

"Did people come and visit and make such a big fuss over me?" asked Sunhi.

"Oh, even more!" said Halmoni. "What a fuss we all made!

"Don't you remember the pictures of your first birthday? I was in Korea, but your parents sent me a big batch of pictures of you every week.

"For your birthday, I made you an outfit and mailed it to your mother."

"I remember those pictures," said Sunhi.

"Now that you are a big sister," said Halmoni, "I thought you could host Kiju's birthday party.

"You, Jenny, and Robin can decorate the birthday table and host together. Why don't you invite them over? We can give them their presents," said Halmoni.

Sunhi nodded.

"Okay, I'll ask them to come home with me tomorrow," she said. "Where is Kiju?"

Halmoni smiled. "I think he is sleeping. Let's go see."

3. A Bad Older Sister

Halmoni and Sunhi walked to Sunhi's parents' room. They peered into Kiju's crib.

Kiju was wide awake and playing happily with his feet. He was a peaceful, handsome baby.

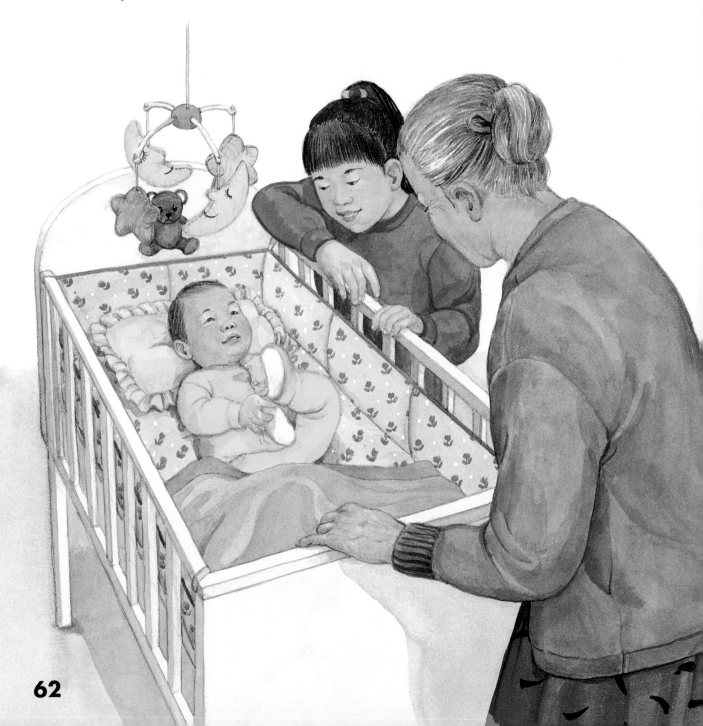

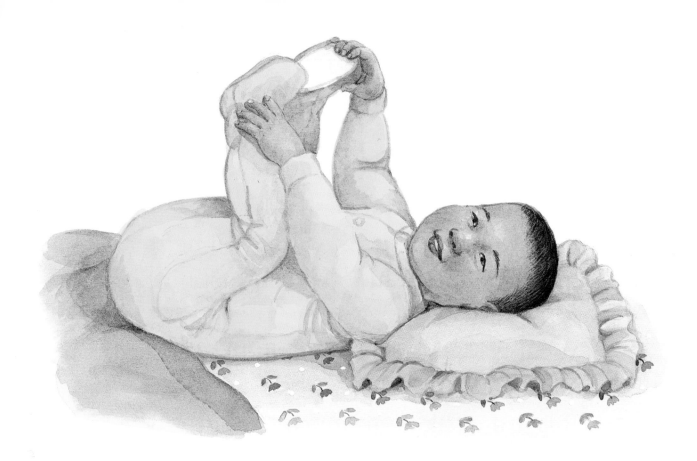

"Kiju is lucky to have a big sister like you," said Halmoni.

"Soon he will be walking and talking. He will follow you all around. You will have to teach him to be smart and kind just like you."

Sunhi's face turned red.

"Halmoni, I was stupid and mean. Sometimes I wanted to be an only child again. I have been a bad older sister," said Sunhi.

"Sunhi, that is all right," said Halmoni. "It is hard to get used to having a baby in the house.

"Sometimes we wish things had not changed. But that doesn't mean we are bad. I know that you love Kiju very much. I know you are going to be the best older sister."

Sunhi watched Kiju. She promised herself that she would give him the best first birthday party ever.

"What is Kiju's birthday outfit like?" asked Sunhi.

"It is just a silk outfit much like the one you wore," said Sunhi's mother, walking into the room.

"He is not wearing an extra-special outfit? He isn't more special and important because he is a boy?" asked Sunhi.

"Of course not! You are both equally special," said Sunhi's mother.

She hugged Sunhi.

Halmoni took Sunhi's hand in her own. She said, "Is your right eye more special and important than your left eye?"

Halmoni had lots of funny sayings like this, but Sunhi understood.

Sook Nyul Choi

"I have always loved books," says Sook Nyul Choi. "As a young girl growing up in Korea, I loved collecting books." Ms. Choi began writing poems and stories as a girl. She found that writing let her share her "thoughts, ideas, and feelings."

Seeing A NEW Sister

by E. Alma Flagg

Baby sister doesn't know
What's going on at all;
How will I ever play with her?
She is so soft and small.

How can I even talk to her?
She only sleeps and sleeps;
But I suppose we'll get along—
They say she's here for keeps.

Reader Response

Let's Talk
Have you ever felt left out like Sunhi? What did you do about it?

Let's Think
Halmoni says, "Is your right eye more special and important than your left eye?" What does she mean?

Test Prep
Let's Write
Pretend that you are Sunhi. Write in your journal about your day. Tell about the lessons you learned.

Make an Invitation

Sunhi will host Kiju's party. Pretend that you will be the host of a party. Make an invitation for your party.

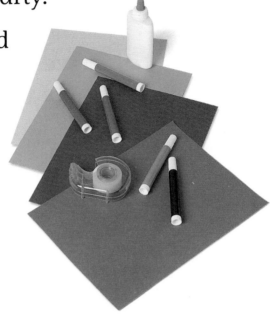

1. Think of a party you would like to host.
2. Make an invitation. Write
   - The day of the party
   - The time
   - Where it will be
   - The reason for the party
3. Draw pictures.
4. Share your invitation with classmates.

You Are Invited

A Party
for: Sarah
day: Saturday, August 2
time: 12:00 p.m.
where: 703 Elm
reason: 9th Birthday

Language Arts

Adjectives

An **adjective** describes a noun. An adjective may tell how something looks, feels, sounds, tastes, or smells.

Grandpa mixes the **crisp, green** salad.

The baby gives a **loud** cry.

The girl drinks **sour** lemonade.

Talk

Tell about the picture. Use adjectives that tell how something looks, feels, sounds, tastes, or smells.

Write

Write these sentences. Use adjectives from the box to finish each sentence.

It was a _____ day. Everyone came to the picnic. We had a lot to eat. The _____ hamburgers were good. The games were fun. We played with a _____ ball.

adjectives		
salty	soft	hot
round	blue	sunny

Write your own sentences about a party. Leave spaces for adjectives. Ask a friend to write an adjective in each space.

Treasure Pie

by Toby Speed   illustrated by Susan Swan

Moose read the note.

Dear Moose,
    Will you come for breakfast today? My pen pal, Bear, is here to visit. She is making her special dish called Treasure Pie. Come to my house at 9:00. Bring bread.
        Your friend,
        Dog

Moose got ready and went to Goat's house.

"I got a note too," said Goat. "Mine says to bring bread. But what is in Treasure Pie?"

"I don't know," said Moose. "Maybe Bear would put in ants."

"Ants!" said Goat and Moose. "Yuck!"

"What would you use instead of ants?" said Moose.

"Twigs!" said Goat.

"Grass!" said Moose.

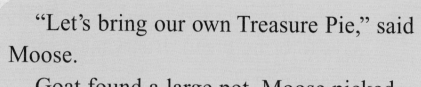

"Let's bring our own Treasure Pie," said Moose.

Goat found a large pot. Moose picked grass. Goat found twigs and spread them out on the table.

"I'll be the washer," said Moose. He began to wash the grass.

"Go ahead," said Goat. "I'll be the cutter."

Moose turned on the oven. "Now for the bread," he said.

"I'm a good baker and mixer," said Goat.

Goat measured and mixed. He put the pan in the oven and set the timer. Soon the bread was ready.

"You are a very good baker," said Moose.

Then they got ready to go to Dog's house.

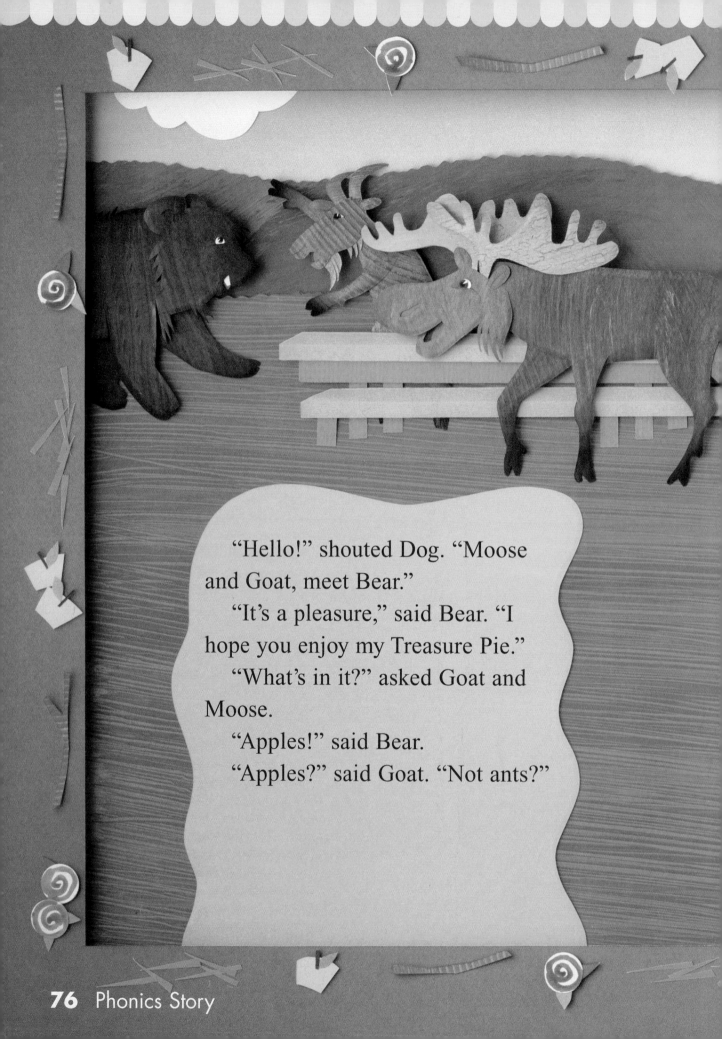

"Hello!" shouted Dog. "Moose and Goat, meet Bear."

"It's a pleasure," said Bear. "I hope you enjoy my Treasure Pie."

"What's in it?" asked Goat and Moose.

"Apples!" said Bear.

"Apples?" said Goat. "Not ants?"

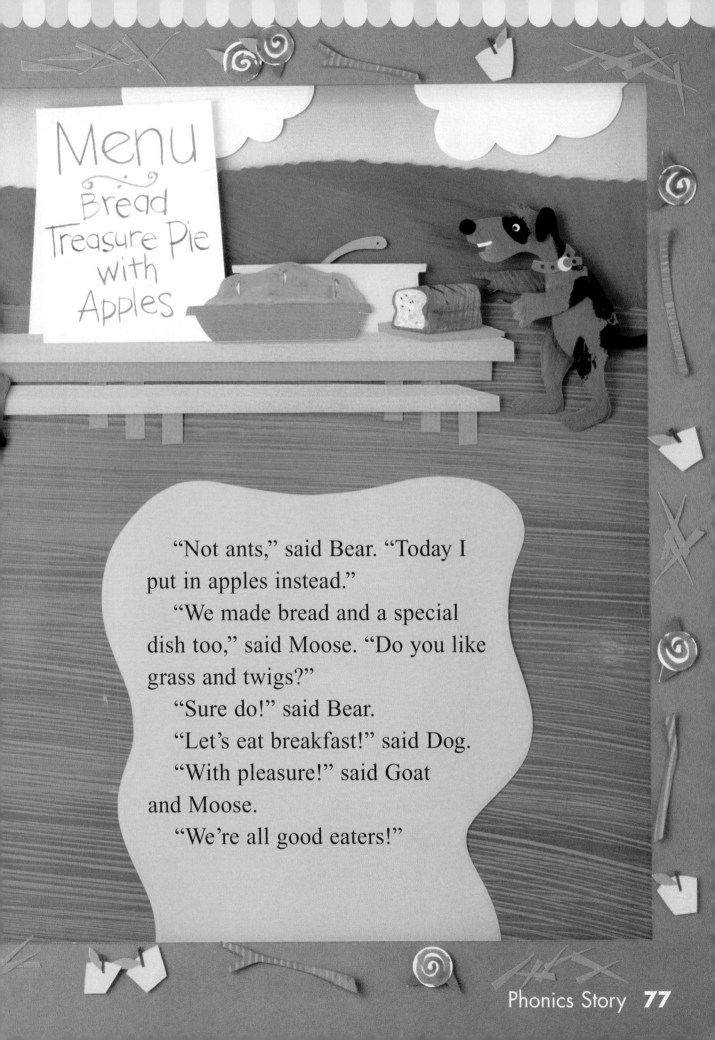

"Not ants," said Bear. "Today I put in apples instead."

"We made bread and a special dish too," said Moose. "Do you like grass and twigs?"

"Sure do!" said Bear.

"Let's eat breakfast!" said Dog.

"With pleasure!" said Goat and Moose.

"We're all good eaters!"

BRUNO
the Baker

by Lars Klinting

Who is that knocking on Bruno's window?
It's Felix. He has a present for Bruno.
Today is Bruno's birthday.

Bruno loves Felix's flowers. He wonders
if Felix would like to stay for some
birthday cake.

Well, first we have to make it!

Here is Bruno's kitchen. He has lots
of pots and pans. Bruno's grandma gave
them to him.

She was a good cook.

What are Bruno and Felix looking for?

Aha! Felix found it—Grandma's cookbook.

Bruno and Felix check the cupboard to see if they have all the ingredients for the cake recipe. They do. Now it's time to get started.

First Bruno melts the butter in a pan.

Next he takes out
the bread crumbs,

a basting brush,

and a cake pan.

Bruno brushes the inside of the cake pan
with some of the melted butter. Then Felix
pours some bread crumbs into the pan and
shakes it so that the bread crumbs stick to
the butter. Bruno turns on the oven.

Now it's time to take out the

sugar,   eggs,   and Bruno's favorite
old bowl.

Bruno cracks the eggs into the bowl. Felix is
a good helper. He adds the sugar.

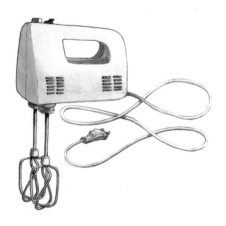

After Bruno stirs together the sugar and eggs, he takes out the electric mixer.

He beats the eggs and sugar until they are fluffy and almost white. Bruno loves this part. Felix thinks it's too noisy.

Bruno is now ready to mix the

baking soda, confectioners' sugar, and flour.

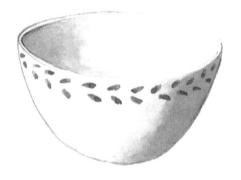

He blends them together in a small bowl.

Felix sets aside the mixing spoon

and the milk.

Bruno pours the milk and the rest of the melted butter into the big bowl with the egg and sugar mixture. Then Felix adds the contents of the small bowl.

Bruno follows the recipe directions carefully. The kitchen is getting a little messy but that's okay.

After Bruno and Felix blend the mixture
well, they pour the batter into the cake pan.
The cake is ready to bake in the oven.

Bruno wears his oven mitts so he won't
get burned.

Felix sets the cake timer. Then Bruno and Felix sit in front of the oven.

The oven has a glass window and a light so they can watch the cake bake.

Pretty soon the kitchen is warm and cozy.

After sitting for a while Bruno and Felix decide to clean up. "Look at the mess we made. We better get to work," says Bruno.

Bruno and Felix wash the dishes while the cake is baking. The kitchen is soon tidy again.

The cake is done. Bruno takes it out of the
oven and lets it cool for a little while.

After it cools, Felix covers the cake with
a doily and places a large plate on top of
the doily.

Then Bruno slips one hand under the cake
pan and holds on to the top as he flips
the cake over. Bruno wiggles the pan a bit
and it comes off. And just look at that cake!
It's perfect!

Now Bruno and Felix take out

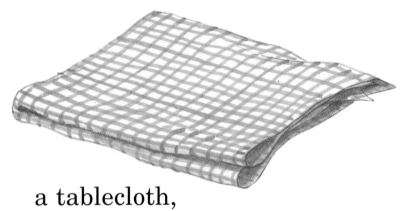

a tablecloth,

a pitcher of juice,

two glasses,

two plates,

two napkins,

and a knife to cut the cake.

Ding-dong!

Just as they finish setting the table
the doorbell rings.

Who can that be?

Happy birthday to you.
Happy birthday to you.
Happy birthday, dear Bruno . . .

"Hurry, Felix! We'll need more plates and
glasses!" says Bruno.

Bruno is happy that his friends have arrived just in time for cake. Everyone agrees that the birthday cake is delicious.

Bruno couldn't have done it without his little buddy, Felix.

What do you think Bruno gets as a present?

A beautiful new mixing bowl!

About the Author
Lars Klinting

Lars Klinting was born in Sweden. He is not only an author but an illustrator. Mr. Klinting has written other Bruno books. He is busy creating another book about Bruno, who can do so many things!

BRUNO'S CAKE

8" x 2" cake pan

$5\frac{1}{8}$ tablespoons butter or
  margarine

1 tablespoon plain bread crumbs,
  finely ground

2 large eggs

1 cup granulated sugar

$1\frac{1}{2}$ cups all-purpose flour, sifted

$1\frac{1}{2}$ teaspoons baking soda

1 tablespoon confectioners' sugar
  (or 1 teaspoon vanilla extract)

$\frac{1}{2}$ cup milk

1. Preheat oven to 350° F.

2. Melt the butter in a pan over a low flame.

3. Brush the cake pan with some of the melted butter.

4. Pour the bread crumbs in the cake pan. Shake it
   carefully so that the crumbs stick to the sides of the
   pan.

5. Beat the eggs and sugar together in a large bowl until
   the mixture is fluffy.

6. Combine the flour, baking soda, and confectioners'
   sugar (or vanilla extract) in a small bowl. Stir well.
   Make sure there are no lumps.

7. Blend milk, remaining butter, and combined flour,
   baking soda, and confectioners' sugar with the egg and
   sugar mixture in the large bowl. Mix until smooth.

8. Pour the batter into the cake pan. Bake for 35
   minutes. Stick a toothpick in the center of the cake.
   If it comes out clean, the cake is done.

9. Let the cake sit for one hour.

To serve the cake as Bruno did: Place a paper
doily on top of cake and then place a large plate
facedown over the doily. Slip one hand under
the cake pan and hold on to the top as you
flip the cake over. Lightly wiggle the pan
free. Sprinkle the top of the cake with
confectioners' sugar.

Yield: 8 pieces of cake.

Reader Response

Let's Talk
Would you like
to plan a party?
Why or why not?

Let's Think
Why is it
important to
make sure you
have everything
before you bake
a cake?

Test Prep
Let's Write
Bruno makes a cake.
What can you make?
Write directions for
someone to follow.

Make a Plan

Today is Bruno's birthday.
Have a party for him. What will you need to do?
Make a plan.

1. Think about your party. What will it be like?

2. Write these questions. Then write your
answers below each question.

- **What will we do?**
- **What will we eat?**
- **How will I decorate?**
- **What other ideas do I have?**

3. Compare your plan
with a classmate's
plan. You may
want to share
some ideas!

Language Arts

Writing with Adjectives

You can use **adjectives** to describe the nouns in your sentences. Adjectives make your sentences clearer and more interesting.

The baker wears a hat.

The **happy** baker wears a **tall** hat.

His helper finds a pan.

His **little** helper finds a **big** pan.

Talk

Pretend you are the cook in the picture. Describe your kitchen and what you are making. Use the list of adjectives.

adjectives		
cozy	sweet	fluffy
messy	white	lumpy
clean	hot	smooth
cold	tasty	large

Write

Write these sentences. Add adjectives to make the sentences clearer and more interesting.

The baker makes a cake in the kitchen. He mixes the batter with a spoon. He pours the batter into a pan. When the cake is finished, he will spread frosting on it.

Write your own sentences about a favorite food. Use adjectives. Ask others if they would like to try your food.

Paul Goes to the Ball

by Eric Kimmel
illustrated by Carolyn Croll

Paul combed his hair. He put on his old coat. He had a fine new coat, but he loved the old one. His own cousin Walter had invited him to a ball. Walter was very rich and Paul was very poor, but they were friends. Paul always had a good story to tell.

Paul walked fast because he wanted to get there early. "Then I'll be able to eat all I want," he thought.

Paul walked to the gate in the wall. He knocked on Walter's door. A tall man came to the door. But he would not let Paul in! He thought Paul was not invited.

"Go away!" said the man. "You can't be a friend of Walter's. All of Walter's friends wear fine clothes."

"But I am Walter's cousin!" Paul cried. "Talk to him! He knows who I am!"

The man shut the door.

Paul walked down the street. "I know what to do," thought Paul. He went home and put on his other coat. Then he walked back to Walter's house.

The same tall man came to the door. He looked at Paul's fine coat. He let him into the hall.

At the ball, Paul saw a table filled with good things to eat. He knew what he would do. He went to the plates and saucers on the table. He put some lamb meat into one pocket of his coat. He put cake into the other pocket. He was able to fill all the pockets of the coat with food.

"Paul, welcome to the ball! But what are you doing?" Walter asked. "Why aren't you eating? Why are you putting all the food into your coat? It looks as if the coat were eating, not you."

"I have a story to tell you, Walter," said Paul. "I came to your house, but I was not welcome because I wore my old coat. So I went home and put on another coat. When I came back wearing this fine coat, I was welcome."

Paul went on. "When you invited me to the ball, I thought you wanted me to come. I was wrong. You wanted someone in a fine coat. You really invited the coat. So I say let the coat eat!"

Walter thought a bit. He said, "I am sorry. You are my friend, not the coat. Come. Sit, eat, talk. Tell me and my friends another story. After all, a coat might eat, but it can't tell a good story."

The Rooster
Who Went to His Uncle's Wedding

A LATIN AMERICAN FOLKTALE

retold by Alma Flor Ada
illustrated by Kathleen Kuchera

Early one morning, when the sun had not yet appeared, the rooster of this story was busy shining his beak and combing up his feathers. It was the day of his uncle's wedding, and the rooster wanted to be on time.

When everything looked perfect he set off
down the road with a brisk and springy walk.
With each step the rooster nodded his head,
thinking of all the wonderful things waiting
for him at the wedding banquet.

Before long his stomach began to growl. "I wish I'd eaten breakfast," he said. Then something caught his eye. There, next to the road, sat a single golden kernel of corn.

Perfect, the rooster thought. But when he got closer he could see that the kernel was lying in a puddle of mud. If he ate it he would get his beak all dirty.

Oh, that rooster was hungry. But he couldn't go to his uncle's wedding with a dirty beak. *What to do? Peck or not peck?* he wondered.

The rooster stared at the kernel.

Then with one sharp peck he gobbled it down
. . . and wound up with a beak full of mud.

So the rooster looked around quickly for someone who could help him. First he noticed the grass growing on the side of the road.

The rooster said to the grass:
"Dear grass, velvety grass,
won't you please clean my beak
so that I can go to my own uncle's wedding?"
But the grass answered:
"No, I won't. Why should I?"

The rooster looked around to
see if there was anyone else who
could help him. Just then he saw
a lamb grazing in the field. Maybe
he could *scare* the grass into
helping. So he asked the lamb:

  "Dear lamb, woolly lamb,
  please eat the grass
  that won't clean my beak
  so that I can go to my own uncle's wedding."
But the lamb answered:
"No, I won't. Why should I?"

The rooster strutted back and forth in dismay. But then he saw a dog walking on the road. So he asked the dog:

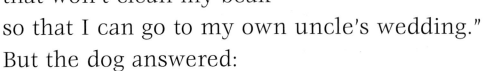

"Dear dog, fierce dog,
please bite the lamb
that won't eat the grass
that won't clean my beak
so that I can go to my own uncle's wedding."
But the dog answered:
"No, I won't. Why should I?"

Well, this rooster was not one to
give up. So he went over to a stick
lying by the road. And he asked it:
    "Dear stick, hard stick,
    please hit the dog
    that won't bite the lamb
    that won't eat the grass
    that won't clean my beak
    so that I can go to my own uncle's wedding."
But the stick answered:
"No, I won't. Why should I?"

The rooster was starting to worry. But he
looked around for someone else to help, and he
spotted a campfire the shepherds had lit. He got
close to the fire and asked:

"Dear fire, bright fire,
please burn the stick
that won't hit the dog
that won't bite the lamb
that won't eat the grass
that won't clean my beak
so that I can go to my own uncle's wedding."
But the fire answered:
"No, I won't. Why should I?"

The rooster ruffled his feathers and paced. Would anyone be able to help him in time? Then he noticed a brook crossing the field. He bent over and whispered, as sincerely as he could:

"Dear water, clear water,
please put out the fire
that won't burn the stick
that won't hit the dog
that won't bite the lamb
that won't eat the grass
that won't clean my beak
so that I can go to my own uncle's wedding."
But the water answered:
"No, I won't. Why should I?"

Now the poor rooster couldn't think of anyone else to ask for help. He lifted his muddy beak up and crowed. But then he noticed that the sun was beginning to appear among the clouds. And he said:

"Dear sun, my good friend,
please dry out the water
that won't put out the fire
that won't burn the stick
that won't hit the dog
that won't bite the lamb
that won't eat the grass
that won't clean my beak
so that I can go to my own uncle's wedding."
And the sun answered:

"Of course I will. Every morning you greet me with your bright song, my friend. I will gladly dry out the water."

But then the water cried out:
"No, please don't dry me out. I will put out
the fire."

And the fire cried out:
"No, please don't put me out. I will burn the stick."

The stick, in turn, cried out:
"No, please don't burn me. I will hit the dog."

But the dog cried out:
"No, please don't hit me. I will bite the lamb."

So the lamb quickly cried out:
"No, please don't bite me. I will eat the grass."

But the grass cried out very loudly:

"No, please don't eat me. I will clean the rooster's beak."

And before you know it the rooster's beak shone as bright as the day.

So the rooster said good-bye to everyone with a happy "Cock-a-doodle-doo!" and went on his way to his uncle's wedding. And he walked with a brisk and springy walk, to get there on time for the banquet.

About the Author
Alma Flor Ada

Alma Flor Ada grew up in a family of storytellers. Her grandmother, father, and uncle told her many tales. "It is not a surprise that I like to tell stories," says Ms. Ada. Ms. Ada's grandmother told her the story of "The Rooster Who Went to His Uncle's Wedding."

Reader Response

Let's Talk

Have you ever needed help from someone else? Tell about it.

Let's Think

What happens when the sun agrees to help? Why?

Test Prep
Let's Write

Pretend that the sun did not help the rooster. Write a new ending for the story.

Make a Story Map

Draw a picture that shows the characters, setting, problem, and solution of the story.

1. Fold a sheet of paper into four parts.
2. Write one of these headings on each part.

   Character   Setting   Problem   Solution

3. Draw pictures for each part.
4. Retell the story to others. Use the story map.

Language Arts

Adjectives with -er and -est

Use adjectives when you compare nouns. Add **-er** to an adjective when you compare two nouns. Add **-est** when you compare more than two nouns.

The blue present is **big.**
The red present is **bigger** than the blue present.
The yellow present is the **biggest** of all.

Talk

Talk about the picture. What is big, short, or tall? Add **-er** or **-est** to compare two or more nouns.

Write

Write these sentences. Choose an adjective with **-er** or **-est**.

1. The_____ candle is blue.
(smaller, smallest)
2. The pig is_____ than the mouse.
(bigger, biggest)

Write sentences of your own. Use an adjective to compare three people, places, or things. Remember to add **-er** or **-est.** Draw a picture to go with your sentences.

Yawning Dawn

by Helen Lester

Dawn was not a morning person. Her family really should have named her Eve, or at least Afternoon.

Dawn often stayed up really late at night, so she was slow to get up in the morning. Her family said that it took her forever to wriggle into her clothes. Each day she barely made the school bus.

It was Friday morning. Mrs. Chipper called the whole class to the big rug. This was the sign for the class to share their writing. Bill read his paper on the new boots he had bought. Missy read her paper on spiders and gnats. Finally it was Dawn's turn.

Dawn yawned. That's when it happened. She yawned and gulped. Then she tried to talk. Instead she BUZZED. Everyone thought it was a fire drill and lined up. But it wasn't really a fire drill buzz, so the whole class came back to the rug.

"Go on, Dawn," said Mrs. Chipper.

Dawn tried to talk. Instead she BUZZED. All the kids thought it was morning recess and put on their coats. But it wasn't really a recess buzz, so the whole class came back to the rug.

"Go on, Dawn," said Mrs. Chipper.

Dawn tried to talk. She BUZZED again!
Mrs. Chipper thought it was the phone.
   "Hello? Hello?" she said. "Who is it?"
But it was not the phone. Everyone finally
saw that it was Dawn who was buzzing.

"Dawn, dear," said Mrs. Chipper. "The bad news is that you buzz. The good news is that you can be your own alarm clock!"

"My own alarm clock!" thought Dawn. "Forever?"

Dawn wailed. Out flew the fly. The whole class saw the fly buzz away.

Dawn shared the paper she wrote. It was about staying up late. But she changed the ending. Now it said that if you stay up late it is hard to get up in the morning. That night Dawn finally went to bed early.

MISSING: One Stuffed Rabbit

by Maryann Cocca-Leffler

It was Friday afternoon, and everyone in the second grade was excited. Coco, the class pet, would spend the whole weekend with one of them!

The classroom grew quiet as Mrs. Robin picked a name.

"Coco will be going home with . . . Janine!" she called.

Janine ran up and gathered Coco and his diary in her arms.

Coco was not a real rabbit. He was a brown stuffed rabbit. He was an important part of Mrs. Robin's second-grade class.

Each day someone's name was picked from a big bowl, and that child got to take Coco home overnight.

Coco traveled everywhere with his diary. Each student helped him write his thoughts inside.

Monday:

I went home with Addie.
I met her bunny, Snowball.
He did not look like me.
Addie ~~red~~ read me Peter Rabbit.
It was a great story.

Tuesday:

I went to the playground
with Danny after school. We
played on the monkey bars.
I fell and broke my leg.
Danny fixed it.

Wednesday:
  Matthew put me in his backpack. We went to soccer practice. Matthew let me wear his favorite hat. I cheered when he got a goal!

Thursday:
  After school I went to the roller-skating ~~ring~~ rink with Christina. My leg is broken so I just watched. Christina's sister fed me a jelly sandwich. My fur is sticky!

Janine was beaming when her mom picked her up. "Guess what! I can keep Coco for the whole weekend!"

She slid into the car. Her baby sister, Kristin, tried to grab Coco. "Mine!" she said.

Janine quickly buckled Coco into his seat belt.

That afternoon, Janine took Coco to visit her nana. Nana cut some carrots for him.

That night at home, Janine read Coco a story and tucked him in bed.

On Saturday, Janine
and Coco did everything
together.

On Sunday, the family went to the mall. Coco came too.

They went from store to store, searching for just the right shoes. Finally they each found the perfect pair, along with lots of other things.

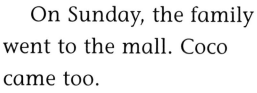

"I'm starving," said Mom. "Let's go for lunch."

They piled their bags into the booth.

"Let's get a highchair for Coco," said Janine. ". . . Coco . . . WHERE'S COCO?"

They looked in all the bags. No Coco. Dad looked under the table. No Coco.

"OH, NO!" cried Janine. "I LOST COCO!"

"Calm down," said Dad. "We'll just retrace our steps."

"Dad, we were in every store in this mall," moaned Janine. "We'll never find him!"

The family spent the rest of the afternoon searching the mall for Coco.

They even checked the Lost and Found Department three times.

On Monday morning, Janine had to go to school without Coco. She stood in front of the class and read from his diary:

Weekend:

I went home with Janine on Friday. On Saturday we rode her bike. On Sunday I got lost in the mall!

Please help Janine find me!

A tear rolled down Janine's cheek.

"Don't worry, Janine—we'll all help," said Mrs. Robin.

"How about if we make posters?" suggested Addie.

"Great idea." Mrs. Robin handed out paper.

MISSING:
ONE STUFFED RABBIT
Name: COCO
Description: brown fur, broken left leg
Lost at the Northshore Mall
Call: Oaklandvale School 555-1234
Lost in
Northshore Mall
Oaklandvale School 555-1234

On Tuesday after school, Mrs. Robin, Janine, and three classmates went to the mall. They hung up all the posters and checked the Lost and Found Department again. No Coco.

As they were leaving, Addie noticed a display. The sign read: "TOY DRIVE. New or good used toys wanted."

Addie and Janine ran to the counter.

"Where do all these toys go?" asked Janine.

"We bring them to the Children's Hospital," said the woman.

"Mrs. Robin!" called Janine. "I'll bet Coco is at the hospital!"

"Let's go!" shouted the children.

They all rushed to the hospital.
As they ran inside, they saw something
amazing. A big green frog was handing
out toys. And poking out of the top of
his basket was one stuffed rabbit—*Coco!*

Just then the frog gave Coco to a
little girl.

"Thank you," said the little girl.
"Look, he has a broken leg just like me!"

"Uh-oh," whispered Janine.

"Isn't he cute?" The little girl held up Coco. "I'm going to name him Cinnamon. I'm going to take care of him."

She gave Coco a big hug. "Cinnamon really needs me."

Janine looked at her friends, then at her teacher.

She cleared her throat.

"I think Coco—I mean, Cinnamon—was lucky to find you."

Janine moved closer to the little girl. "My name is Janine."

"I'm Teresa."

At that moment the frog gathered everyone together for some photos. *SNAP. SNAP.* He gave pictures to Janine and Teresa.

The next morning, Janine stood in front of
the class and held up the picture. She read from
Coco's diary.

Tuesday:
    Janine and the others found me. I am now with someone who really needs me. Her name is Teresa. She loves me and will take good care of me. I had a lot of fun in your class, but I won't be coming back.

                    Love,
                    Coco

P.S. My new name is Cinnamon.
P.P.S. Please write to Teresa and me.

And that's just what they did.

About the Author
Maryann Cocca-Leffler

Maryann Cocca-Leffler wrote *Missing: One Stuffed Rabbit* for her daughters, Janine and Kristen. She also wrote it for Janine's first-grade teacher and classmates.

"All the children got to take Coco home!" writes Ms. Cocca-Leffler about Janine's class.

Ms. Cocca-Leffler's daughter Kristin made the poster illustration of Coco on page 161.

Rosie

by Carol Diggory Shields

Have you met our Rosie yet?
She's very, very sweet.
We love her from her round pink ears
Down to her tiny feet.
Be gentle, you can take her out—
She'll climb up on your shoulder.
And even Jake sits quiet when
He gets a turn to hold her.

Reader Response

Let's Talk

Have you ever owned something special? Tell about it.

Let's Think

Why does Janine let the little girl in the hospital keep Coco?

Test Prep
Let's Write

At the end of the story, Coco asks the class to write to Teresa and to him. Pretend that you are a part of the second-grade class in the story. Write a letter to Coco.

Dear Coco,

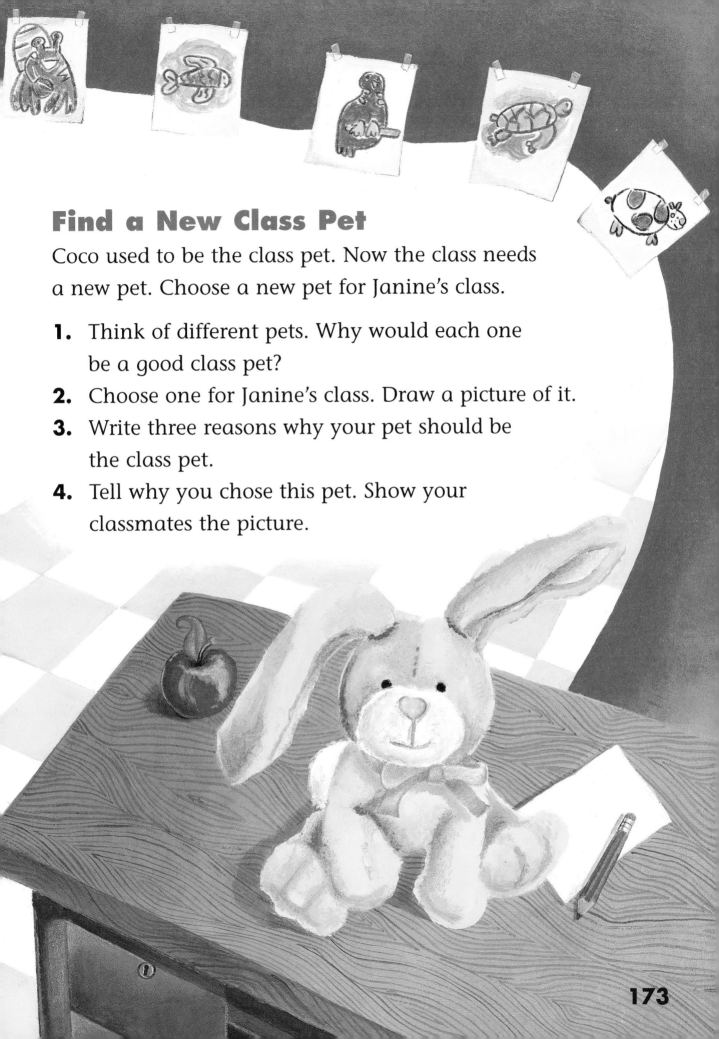

Find a New Class Pet

Coco used to be the class pet. Now the class needs a new pet. Choose a new pet for Janine's class.

1. Think of different pets. Why would each one be a good class pet?
2. Choose one for Janine's class. Draw a picture of it.
3. Write three reasons why your pet should be the class pet.
4. Tell why you chose this pet. Show your classmates the picture.

Adverbs

An **adverb** is a word that tells about a verb. Use an adverb to tell when, where, or how an action takes place.

The bell rings **now.** (when)

The teacher sits **here.** (where)

The children listen **quietly.** (how)

When, where, and how does the action happen?

Talk

Talk about the picture. What else might happen in this classroom? Use the adverbs from the box.

The little rabbit had two big ears.

The little r ate carrot dinner.

adverbs		
when	**where**	**how**
now	here	carefully
soon	inside	happily
early	outside	neatly
always	near	slowly

174

Write

Write these sentences. Circle the adverbs. Then write whether they tell when, where, or how.

1. **The children sit near the teacher.**
2. **The teacher rocks slowly.**
3. **The children will eat soon.**

Write your own sentences. Describe your classroom. Use adverbs that tell when, where, and how.

Birthday Joy

The Best Older Sister

attention

different

important

interesting

secretly

special

told

Hear the Cheers

The Great Ball Game

ago

creature

head

loses

still

team

Treasure Pie

BRUNO
the Baker

kitchen

large

oven

present

ready

today

wash

Yawning Dawn

MISSING:
ONE STUFFED
RabbiT

calm

family

finally

gathered

hospital

morning

paper

really

Paul Goes to
the Ball

The Rooster
Who Went to His Uncle's Wedding

able

brook

early

feathers

growl

own

story

Test Talk

Complete the Sentence

A test may show an incomplete sentence. You must choose the answer that correctly completes the sentence.

A test about *Bruno the Baker* might ask you to complete this sentence.

1. Bruno and Felix used a round pan to bake ___.

(A) a cake

(B) a present

(C) cookies

Read the incomplete sentence. Think about what you need to find out. Then choose the right answer. Make sure it correctly completes the sentence.

Here is how one girl chose her answer.

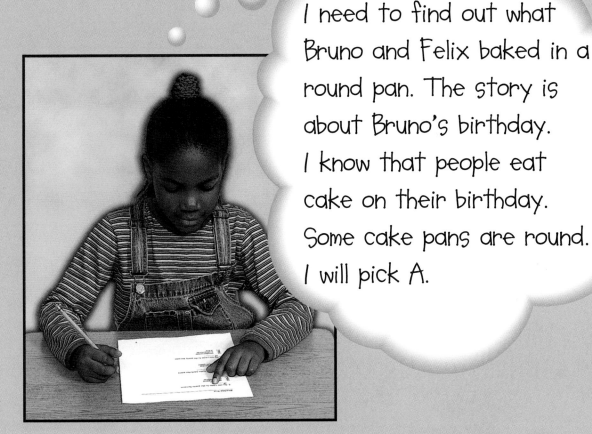

I need to find out what Bruno and Felix baked in a round pan. The story is about Bruno's birthday. I know that people eat cake on their birthday. Some cake pans are round. I will pick A.

Try it!

Use what you have learned to complete this sentence about *Bruno the Baker.*

2. Bruno's friends buy him a new ___ to use in the kitchen.

Ⓐ TV

Ⓑ mixing bowl

Ⓒ hammer

All Aboard!

What can we learn by traveling?

Space Dreams

by Anne Sibley O'Brien illustrated by Larry Johnson

My dad says if I try hard, I can be anything I
want to be. I have a list of all the things I want to
be. I began it when I was five. Here is my list.

1. An astronaut like Sally Ride
2. An inventor like Thomas Edison
3. A cook like my dad

I showed my list to my dad. He said it might be tough, but I could do all those things.

So, while I may be young, I still have very big dreams. I'm going to be an astronaut who invents a spaceship and cooks all different foods on it. I began to get ideas for my spaceship when I was watching TV.

My dad and I were watching a program about the first trip to the moon. He could remember when the capsule touched down.

"I was just your age," Dad said. "When your grandfather was that young, he didn't dream that a person would ever try to walk on the moon."

Ever since I saw this program, I knew space travel was for me.

My spaceship will travel around Earth. It will have a big table in the middle of it. Astronauts from all different countries will eat together.

Every night we will all cook a dish from another country. After dinner, we will talk for a long time. At the touch of a button, everything will be cleaned up. It will be no trouble at all.

Here are some of the things on my spaceship:

1. Books from different countries
2. Enough games for everyone to play
3. Windows everywhere

People will have enough time to read and play games. They will become friends.

From the spaceship they will look out the windows. They will see the beautiful blue and green Earth. They will remember that we all share this planet together.

Man on the Moon

by Anastasia Suen
illustrated by Benrei Huang

Moon,
do you remember
your first visitors?

It was 1969 . . .
Astronauts Collins, Aldrin,
and Armstrong suited up.

Each had flown in space, but no one had
ever touched the moon.
No one.

Some said it couldn't be done. Astronauts Collins,
Aldrin, and Armstrong were going to try.

Into *Apollo 11* they climbed.
The countdown began.
3-2-1 and . . .

"Liftoff! Liftoff!
Apollo 11
has cleared the tower!"

Saturn 5 shot them into the sky.

Around the Earth they flew as
the rockets dropped off, then
whoosh! straight
for the moon. . . .

Hours and days passed.
The people on Earth
watched the astronauts on TV.

Over and over the capsule turned.

Suddenly, the sky went dark.

It was the moon!
For the first time,
Apollo 11 saw the moon.

The astronauts circled, looking for a place to land.
In the morning, their spacecraft would separate.

Columbia, named after Columbus,
would sail around the moon.
The *Eagle,* like a bird, would fly there.

The next day,
Aldrin and Armstrong
climbed into the *Eagle*.

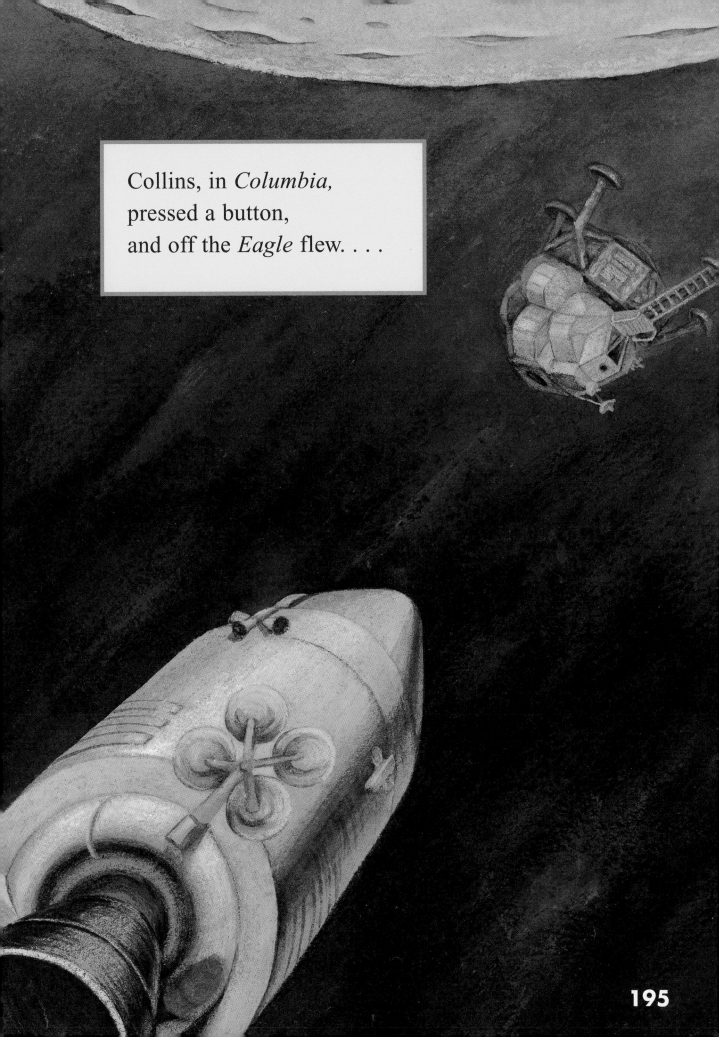

Collins, in *Columbia*,
pressed a button,
and off the *Eagle* flew. . . .

Buttons and gadgets,
switches and lights!
Alarms rang again and again.

In the control room, Houston said, "Go."
The *Eagle* flew on.

On the moon,
craters loomed.
The *Eagle* was going too fast!

Armstrong took the controls
and began to fly.
Houston and the Earth waited.

Fifty feet . . . thirty feet . . .
Contact!

"Houston,
Tranquility Base here.
The *Eagle* has landed."

With cameras rolling,
as millions watched,
Astronaut Neil Armstrong touched the moon.

"That's one small step for man," he said,
"one giant leap for mankind."

Aldrin and Armstrong
took pictures, collected rocks,
and planted the American flag.

Hours later,
the *Eagle* left the moon
and linked up with *Columbia*.

Home again,
Collins, Aldrin, and Armstrong
splashed down in the Pacific Ocean.

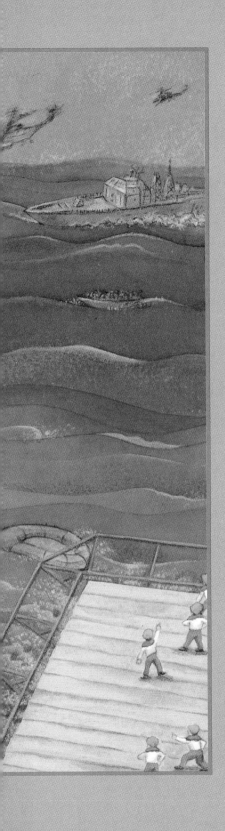

Some said it couldn't be done. Mike Collins, Buzz Aldrin, and Neil Armstrong proved them wrong . . .

and made history.

Glossary

Words from *Man on the Moon*

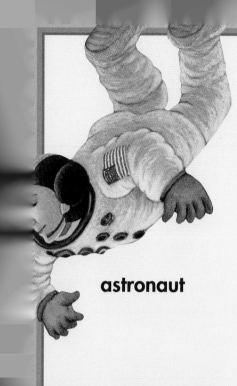

astronaut

astronaut
: a person who rides in a spacecraft

capsule
: the front part of a rocket

controls
: buttons and other tools for operating a spacecraft

countdown
: the calling out of the seconds left before a spacecraft lifts off

crater

crater
: a hole in the ground that is shaped like a bowl

gadget
: a small tool

liftoff
: the raising into the air of a rocket or spacecraft

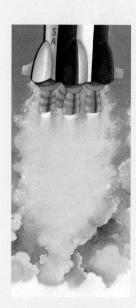

liftoff

spacecraft
: something astronauts ride in to travel in space

About the Author

Anastasia Suen

When Anastasia Suen was a child, her family lived in Florida. "I grew up with NASA" (the National Aeronautics and Space Administration, which directs the U.S. space program), says Ms. Suen. She and her brother watched from their backyard as rockets took off into space. She watched the *Eagle*'s moon landing on TV with her family.

Reader Response

Let's Talk

If you were going to the moon, what part of the trip would you look most forward to?

Let's Think

The author says, "Some said it couldn't be done." What does she mean?

Test Prep
Let's Write

Pretend you are an astronaut on the moon. Send a postcard to your family and friends. Write about your trip.

Interview an Astronaut

If you could interview Neil Armstrong, what questions would you ask?

1. Write five questions to ask Neil Armstrong. Ask a friend to pretend to be Neil Armstrong and answer the questions.
2. Practice asking the questions. Listen to the answers.
3. When you are ready, get a tape recorder. Record your interview.
4. Play the tape for your classmates.

Pronouns

A **pronoun** is a word that takes the place of a noun or nouns. **I, he, she, it, we,** and **they** are pronouns.

The boy dreams in his bedroom.
He dreams in his bedroom.

The rocket takes off.
It takes off.

The astronauts land on the moon.
They land on the moon.

Use the pronoun **I** in place of your name.

I love space!

Talk

Find people, places, or things in the picture. Name the noun. Tell what pronoun to use in place of each noun.

Write

Write these sentences. Change the underlined nouns to pronouns.

1. The astronauts could see <u>the moon</u> out their window.

2. <u>Grandma and I</u> like to read books about the moon.

Write your own story. Use pronouns in place of some nouns. Begin with this sentence:

Someday I will go to the moon with my friend.

Two Lunches
at the Mill

by Kana Riley

illustrated by Miles Hyman

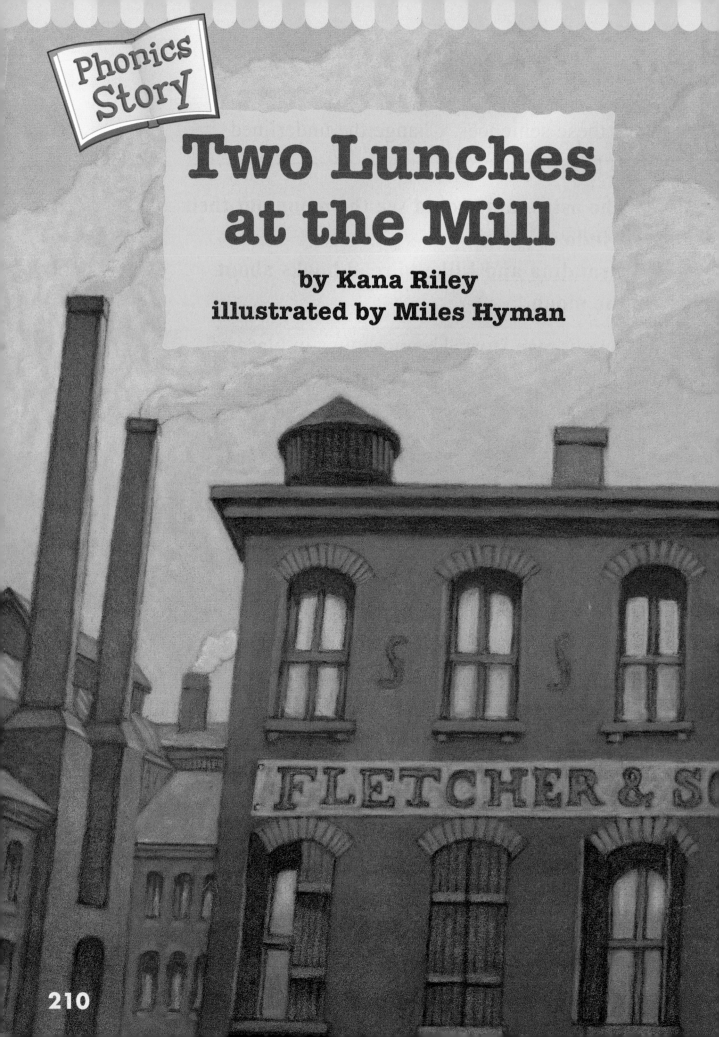

Bong! Bong! Above us, the bell in the mill tower begins to ring. "Lunch time!" says my grandma. I call her Gran.

Gran's humble family once worked in the cloth mill.

"The bell in the tower was our family clock," Gran says. "At noon, when the bell rang, we knew it was time to eat. Mama would pack lunches for everyone.

"My sister Jenny would walk across the street to the mill with the lunch boxes. People from all the houses did the same thing. One day I went along with Jenny. She carried boxes of sandwiches for our big sisters. I carried only one. It was for Papa. I walked along behind Jenny.

"She opened the door to a big room. There stood row upon row of machines. People sat only inches apart upon simple, maple benches. What a rumble of noises! There were clashes and hisses all around.

"Jenny ran ahead. I looked around. I called for her. But no one could hear a word I said.

"So I scrambled out the door . . . right into Papa!

" 'You brought sandwiches,' he said. 'And peaches . . . and an apple! You sure are a good girl!'

"After that, I carried his lunch every day," says Gran. "Soon I knew my way around all the places in the mill."

Gran looks at the dresses in the shop windows as we walk. "Upon my word," she says, "what pretty red sashes."

Then she turns to me. "Now, young man, I'm sure you're as hungry as Papa ever was. Let's find a table and order our lunches."

"Sure, Gran," I say.

Going to TOWN

adapted from
Little House in the Big Woods

by Laura Ingalls Wilder
illustrated by Renée Graef

Once upon a time, a little
girl named Laura lived in
the Big Woods of Wisconsin in
a little house made of logs.

She lived in the little house with her Pa, her Ma, her big sister Mary, her baby sister Carrie, and their good old bulldog Jack.

One day Pa said that as soon as he had finished planting the crops, they would all go to town. Laura, Mary, and Carrie could go too. They were old enough now.

Laura and Mary were very excited! The next day they tried to play going to town. They could not do it very well, because they were not sure what a town was like. They had never even seen a store.

Then one night Pa said, "We'll go to town tomorrow." That night Ma gave Laura and Mary a bath. Then she wound their wet hair tightly on lots of little rags. In the morning their hair would be curly.

When Laura and Mary woke up, they put on their best dresses. Mary buttoned up the back of Laura's red calico dress, and Ma buttoned up the back of Mary's blue calico dress. Then Ma took the rags out of their hair and combed it into long round curls that hung down over their shoulders.

After breakfast Pa drove the wagon up to the gate of the little house. He had brushed the horses until they shone. Ma sat up on the wagon seat with Pa, holding Baby Carrie in her arms. Laura and Mary sat behind Ma and Pa on the board across the wagon box. They were going to town!

They were happy as they rode through the springtime woods. Ma was smiling, Carrie laughed and bounced, and Pa whistled while he drove the horses. Rabbits stood up in the road ahead, and the sun shone through their tall ears. Twice Laura and Mary saw deer looking at them with their large, dark eyes among the trees.

Suddenly Pa stopped the horses and pointed ahead with his whip. "There you are, Laura and Mary!" he said. "There's the town of Pepin."

Laura had never imagined so many houses and so many people. There were more houses than she could count. Laura looked and looked, and could not say a word.

Pa helped everyone down from the wagon, and they walked up to the biggest building in town. This was the store where Pa came to trade. As they climbed up the steps of the store, Laura was so excited that she was trembling all over.

The store was full of things to look at. There were sacks of salt and sugar. There were pink and blue and red and brown and purple fabrics for dresses. There were boots and hammers and nails and big wooden pails full of candy. There were so many things that Laura did not know how Pa and Ma could ever choose.

When all the trading was done, the storekeeper gave Mary and Laura each a piece of candy. They were so surprised that they just stood looking at their candies. Then they remembered and said, "Thank you." The candies were shaped like hearts and had printing on them. Mary's candy said:

> *Roses are red,*
> *Violets are blue,*
> *Sugar is sweet,*
> *And so are you.*

Laura's said only:

> *Sweets to the sweet.*

After they left the store, they walked over to the lake at the edge of town. They all sat on the warm sand, and Ma opened the picnic basket that she had brought. Inside there were bread and butter and cheese, hard-boiled eggs, and cookies for lunch.

After the picnic was over, they all got back into the wagon to go home. It was a long trip through the Big Woods to the little house. Laura and Mary were very tired, and Baby Carrie was asleep in Ma's arms. But Pa sang softly:

" 'Mid pleasures and palaces, though
    we may roam,
  Be it ever so humble, there's no place
    like home."

About the Author
Laura Ingalls Wilder

Laura Ingalls was born in a log cabin in 1867. She married Almanzo Wilder, and they had a daughter, Rose. She shared the stories of her life with Rose. Later, Rose convinced her mother to publish her family's stories.

Laura Ingalls Wilder said, "I lived everything that happened in my books."

Reader Response

Let's Talk

How is your life like Laura's? How is it different?

Let's Think

When Laura looks at the houses and people in town, she cannot speak. Why?

Test Prep
Let's Write

Laura takes a trip to town. Think about a trip you have taken or a trip you would like to take. Write about one day in your trip. Describe where you were, what you saw, and what you did.

Plan a Trip

Think of places you have been. Where would you like to go? Make a plan for a trip.

1. Think of a place. It can be real or made-up.
2. Answer these questions on a large sheet of paper.
   Where is it?
   What is it called?
   How will you get there?
   What does it look like?
   Where will you stay?
   What can you do there?
3. Draw a picture of the place.
4. Share your plan with a classmate.

Language Arts

Singular and Plural Pronouns

A **pronoun** is a word that takes the place of a noun or nouns. Pronouns that tell about one person or thing are **singular.**

The teacher writes on the chalkboard. **She** writes on the chalkboard.

Pronouns that tell about more than one person or thing are **plural.**

The students learn to read. **They** learn to read.

singular pronouns	plural pronouns
I	we
you	you
he, she, it	they

Talk

Tell how the classroom in the picture is different from your classroom. Use pronouns from the list.

Write

Write these sentences. Change the underlined words to pronouns.

My sister and I like to learn about the past. A long time ago children went to school in log cabins. <u>The children</u> sat on benches. The school was very small. Only a few people could fit in <u>the school</u>. The school had a teacher. <u>The teacher</u> was very strict. <u>My sister and I</u> would like to visit an old school soon.

Pretend that you and your friends are in the old school. Write sentences about it. Use singular and plural pronouns.

A True Boating Family

by David McPhail

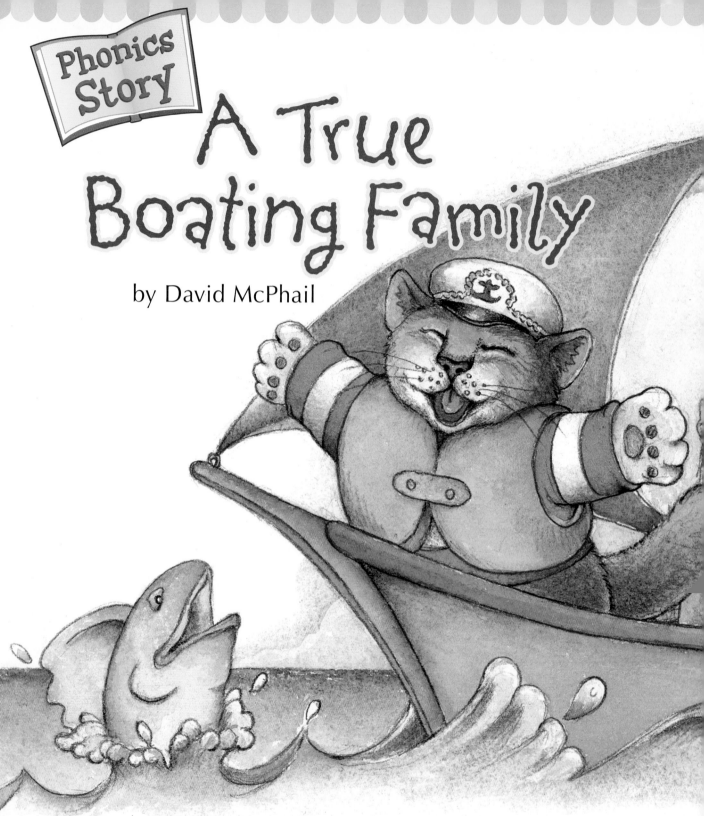

My uncle's boat has big, blue sails.
When he goes by, fish wave their tails.

They jump and seem to sing with him.
My uncle watches as they swim.

My cousin Sue comes on, I hear.
Some days, it's true, she even steers.

My brother has a boat that's small.
He rows it fast, and thrills us all.

He likes to take me. That I know.
He glides through water. See him go!

For years my mother sailed big ships.
She went on many long, long trips.

One ship of hers was called *Sweet Pea.*
It carried things from sea to sea.

Some boxes were red, white, and blue.
They all were full of sticky glue.

My father steers a mighty tug,
which pushes, pulls, and goes
Chug, chug!

He works in every kind of weather.
From time to time, we go together!

Of course, my sister has a boat,
It's tiny, but it sure can float!

Riding the Ferry with Captain Cruz

by Alice K. Flanagan
photographed by Christine Osinski

Hear the horn blow? Hurry! The ferryboat is leaving.

See the captain on deck? That's Mr. Cruz, my neighbor.

All day long, Captain Cruz takes people back and forth from Staten Island to New York City, across the bay.

Before the ferry leaves, the crew
makes sure everything on board works.
The trip must be safe!

Hear the engines hum?

Slowly, Captain Cruz steers the ferry away from the dock.

He checks his
compass to see
which direction
the ferry is going.

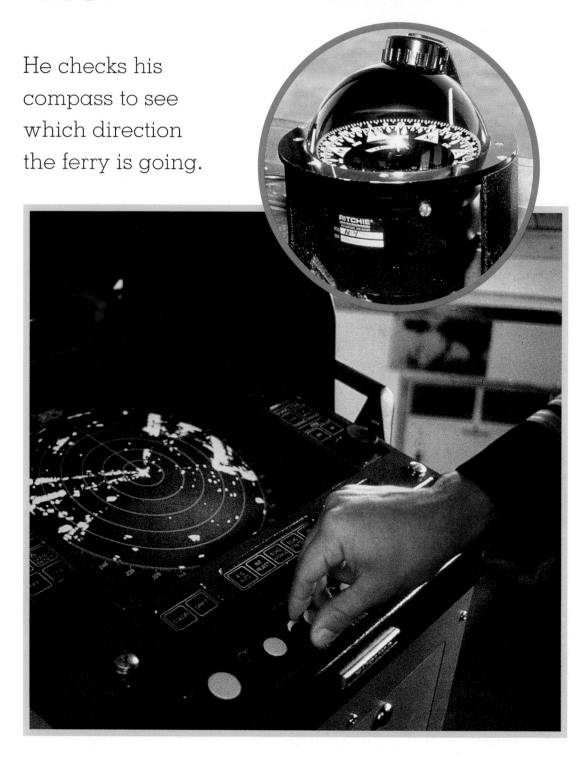

He watches the radar screen. It shows
him how to keep the ferry on course.

Captain Cruz uses a radio to talk with his crew. They are like a family.

A deckhand sits at the captain's side day and night. He is an extra pair of eyes looking out.

Feel the roll of the waves? The captain
handles the ferry well. He has been a
ferryboat captain for ten years.

He knows all about the weather and the water
currents, the bridges and the passing ships,
and the famous Statue of Liberty.

Captain Cruz watches these things each day on his way to and from the city.

Feel the ferry stop?
We have crossed the bay.

After every trip, and at the end of each day, Captain Cruz writes in the captain's log. He records what happened along the way.

The captain does his job well.

He helps people get to work safely and on time.

Captain Cruz is careful and responsible. With hard work, he has made his dream of being a ferryboat captain come true!

About the Author

Alice K. Flanagan grew up in Chicago. She loved telling stories. So did her sister Christine Osinski. They also enjoyed drawing pictures together. Now Alice works with her sister to create books for children.

About the Photographer

Christine Osinski takes the photographs that you see in Alice Flanagan's books. Christine lives in Staten Island, New York. That is where Mr. Cruz is a ferryboat captain.

Barcarola

por Nicolás Guillén
illustrado por Shelly Hehenberger

El mar con sus ondas mece
la barca, mece
la barca junto a la costa
brava, la mece
el mar.

Del hondo cielo la noche
cae, la noche
con su gran velo flotando
cae la noche
al mar!

The Boatman's Song

by Nicolás Guillén
illustrated by Shelly Hehenberger

The waves of the sea
rock the boat,
rock the boat by the shore.
The wild sea
rocks the boat.

Out of the deep sky
the night falls,
the night with its floating veil,
the night falls
into the sea.

257

Reader Response

Let's Talk

Would you like to be a ferryboat captain? What would be the best part? What would be the worst part?

Let's Think

Is Captain Cruz a good captain? How do you know?

Test Prep
Let's Write

Pretend you own a ferryboat. You need a captain. Describe the person you would hire for this job.

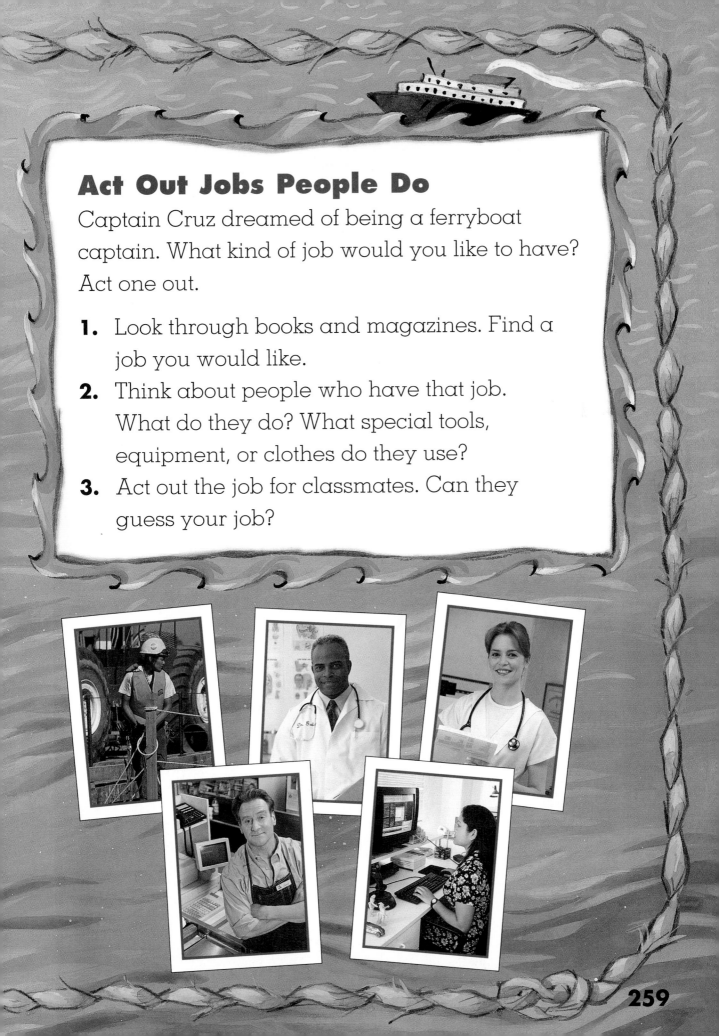

Act Out Jobs People Do

Captain Cruz dreamed of being a ferryboat captain. What kind of job would you like to have? Act one out.

1. Look through books and magazines. Find a job you would like.
2. Think about people who have that job. What do they do? What special tools, equipment, or clothes do they use?
3. Act out the job for classmates. Can they guess your job?

Pronouns Before and After Verbs

Some pronouns are the subject of the sentence. They come before the verb. These pronouns are **I, he, she, we, they**.

The captain steers the ferry.
He steers the ferry.

Some pronouns come after the verb. These pronouns are **me, him, her, us, them.**

The children wave to **the captain.**
The children wave to **him.**

You can use the pronouns **you** and **it** before or after the verb.

Talk

Make up sentences about the picture. Use nouns. Say the sentences again. Use pronouns. Do they come before or after the verb?

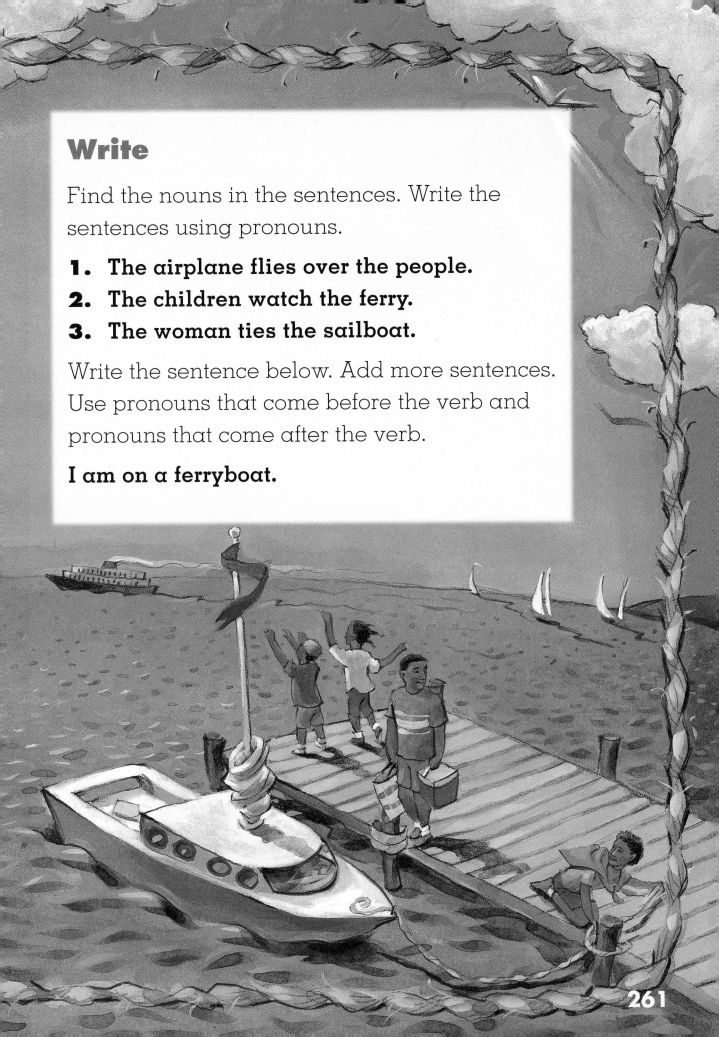

Write

Find the nouns in the sentences. Write the sentences using pronouns.

1. The airplane flies over the people.
2. The children watch the ferry.
3. The woman ties the sailboat.

Write the sentence below. Add more sentences. Use pronouns that come before the verb and pronouns that come after the verb.

I am on a ferryboat.

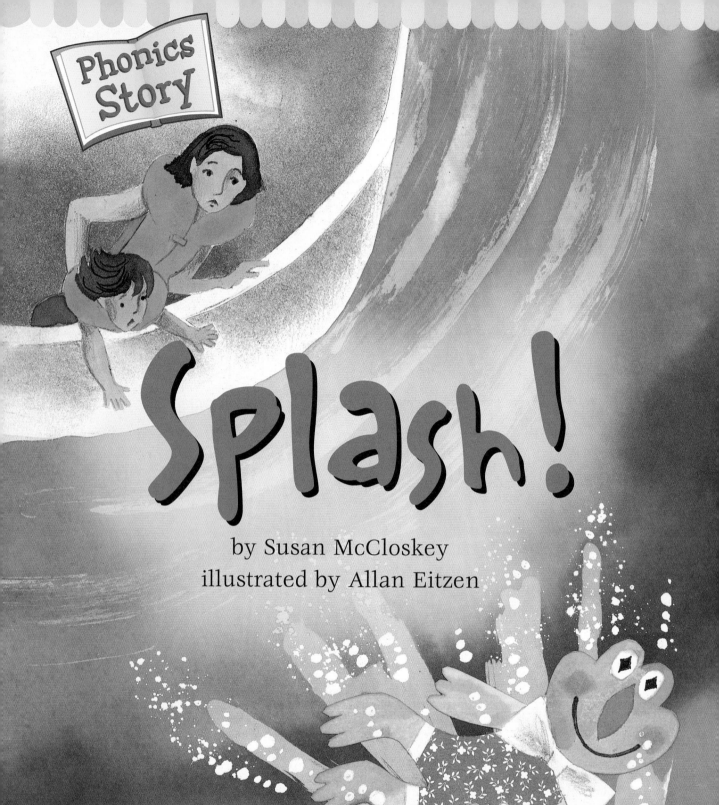

Splash!

by Susan McCloskey
illustrated by Allan Eitzen

Splash!
Oh, no! Poor Blinkie has fallen into the
sea! And the water is terribly cold!

Splash! Splash! Mom and Dad are diving to the rescue!

Now Blinkie is sinking! Mom and Dad would grab him, but they can't move any closer. He's too near that jellyfish. Jellyfish can sting.

Blinkie is under the sea now.

What is making the water grow dark? Oh! An octopus is giving off a cloud of ink. It must be frightened.

The octopus is waving its eight arms. One arm has reined in Blinkie!

The octopus is swimming away! Mom and Dad scared it off.

Oh, no! Where is Blinkie now?

There's Blinkie! A fish is using its weight to push him away. It's a fish that is fussy about its neighbors.

Now Blinkie is at the bottom of the sea.

The beige stone near Blinkie starts to move. Why, it's not a stone at all! It's a stonefish! It has stinging spines on its back. They are filled with poison.

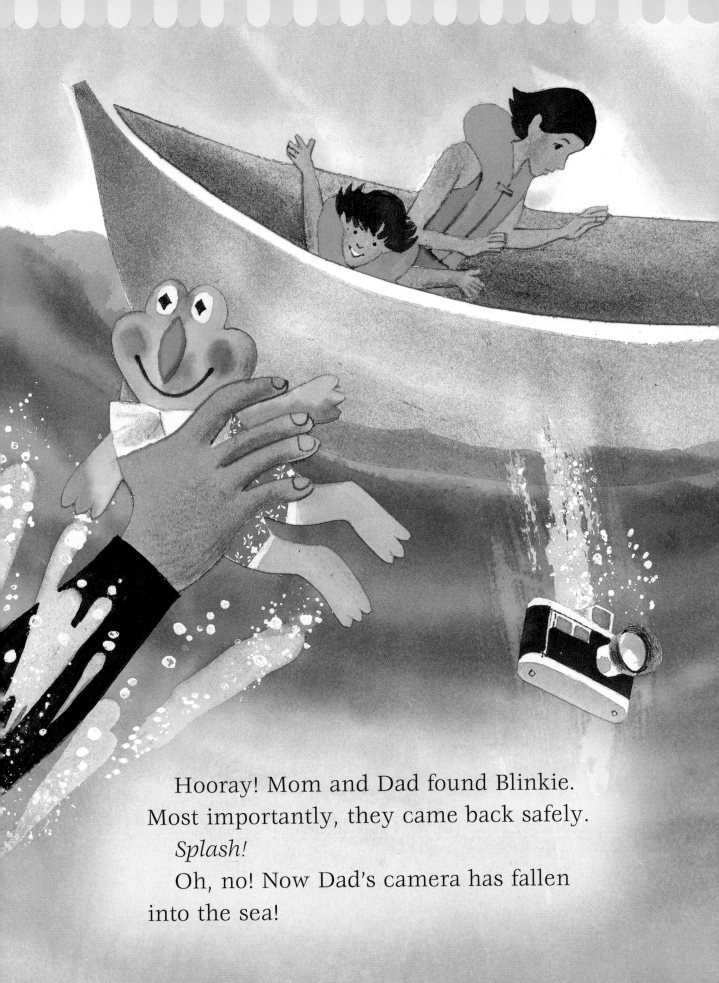

Hooray! Mom and Dad found Blinkie.
Most importantly, they came back safely.
Splash!
Oh, no! Now Dad's camera has fallen
into the sea!

Down in the Sea:
The Jellyfish

by Patricia Kite

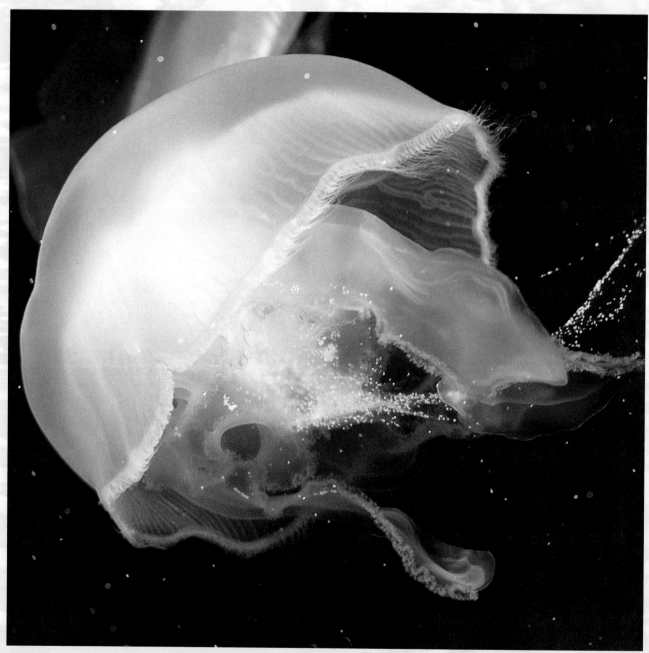

A jiggly jellyfish
is flopped on the beach.
Do not poke it. Ouch!

Soon the sun
dries out the jelly,
which is really mostly water.
The next day,
if you looked,
all you would see is this.

But there are
many more jellyfish
floating in the water,
near, or far, far away.

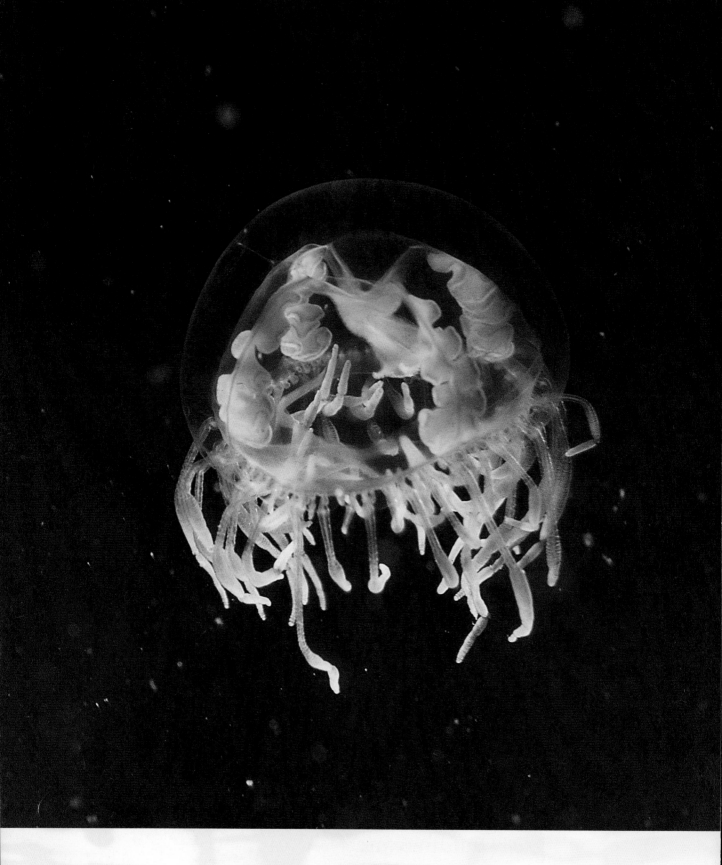

Jellyfish come in many sizes—
smaller than a grape
and bigger than a bed.

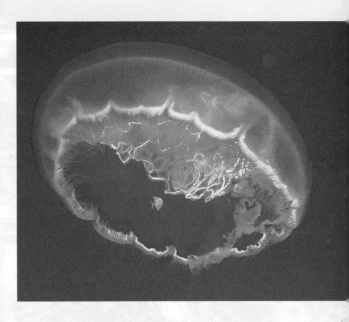

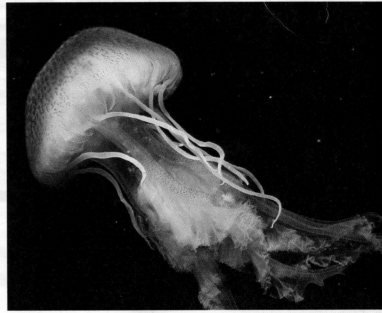

Jellyfish come in many shapes.
Some look like cups.
Some look like bowls.
Some look like parachutes.

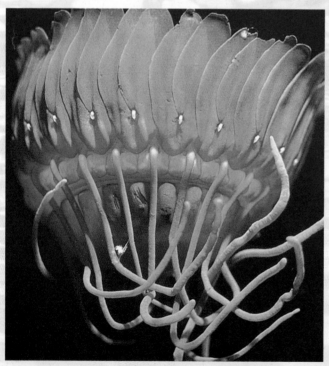

Many jellyfish are see-through,
but they can come in colors—
white, blue, pink, yellow, green,
purple, red, orange, and striped.

Some even light up at night
or in sunless deep water.

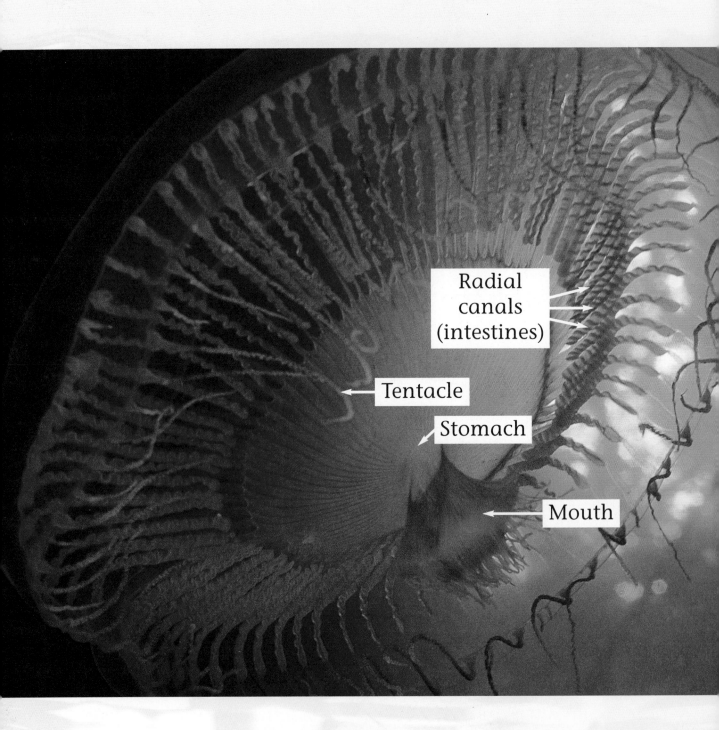

Radial
canals
(intestines)

Tentacle

Stomach

Mouth

Jiggly jellyfish
look like blobs of jelly
around a stomach hole.
All eat a lot.

Jellyfish eat fish, crabs, worms,
shrimp, plankton, plants,
and, sometimes, smaller jellyfish. Yum!
Most jellyfish catch food with tentacles.
Tentacles look like cooked noodles
hanging from under the jellyfish.

Some tentacles are just an inch or less.
But they can be one hundred twenty feet long.
That's longer than a basketball court. Wow!

A jellyfish may have a few tentacles
or as many as eight hundred.

Stingers

Stinging cells

Each tentacle is dotted
with stinging cells.
When food swims by,
it touches a tentacle.
Soon the food no longer moves.
The tentacles pull it
to the jellyfish's mouth.

To move from place to place,
a jellyfish floats or opens
and closes its body like an umbrella.
Opening lets water under the umbrella.
Closing pushes it out like a jet. *Whoosh!*

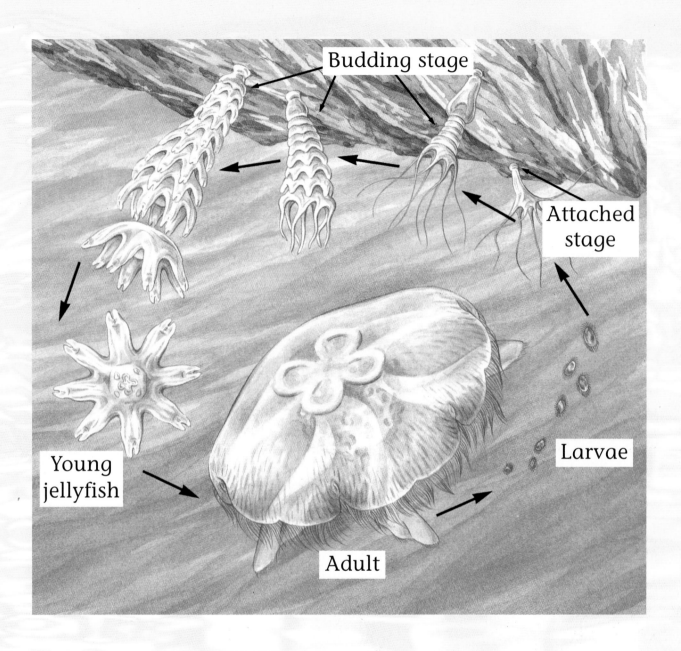

Budding stage

Attached stage

Larvae

Young jellyfish

Adult

Baby jellyfish don't look
like their parents.
At least, not at first.
This is how many jellyfish grow.

Each jellyfish lives about a year,
if a fish or turtle or bird does not
eat it first, and the water is not
too warm or cold.

Jellyfish have been on this earth
a long time (four hundred fifty
million years). There were jellyfish
before there were dinosaurs!

About the Author
Patricia Kite

"I love to make words dance, information sing, and children smile," says Patricia Kite.

Ms. Kite enjoys writing about science. She says she wanted to write about jellyfish because she had always wondered if they "were really made of jelly."

Reader Response

Let's Talk
What facts about the jellyfish surprised you?

Let's Think
What do you think is the most important thing to know about jellyfish? Why?

Test Prep
Let's Write
Pretend you are a jellyfish. Write about a day in your life. Use what you learned to write your story.

Make a Jellyfish

Jellyfish come in many shapes, colors, and sizes. Make your own jellyfish.

1. Draw your jellyfish.
2. Plan what you will need to make the body and the tentacles. Get materials.
3. Make your jellyfish.
4. Hang your jellyfish in the room for classmates to see.

Writing with Pronouns

Pronouns can be the subject of a sentence or come after the verb.

The divers like to look for jellyfish.
They like to look for jellyfish.

The fish saw **the net.**
The fish saw **it.**

When you write, try not to use the same noun over and over again. Use a pronoun to take the place of a noun.

The divers swim deep in the water.
They find fish.

Talk

Tell a story about the picture. Take turns adding sentences. Try not to use the same noun over and over again. Use pronouns in the subject of a sentence or after the verb.

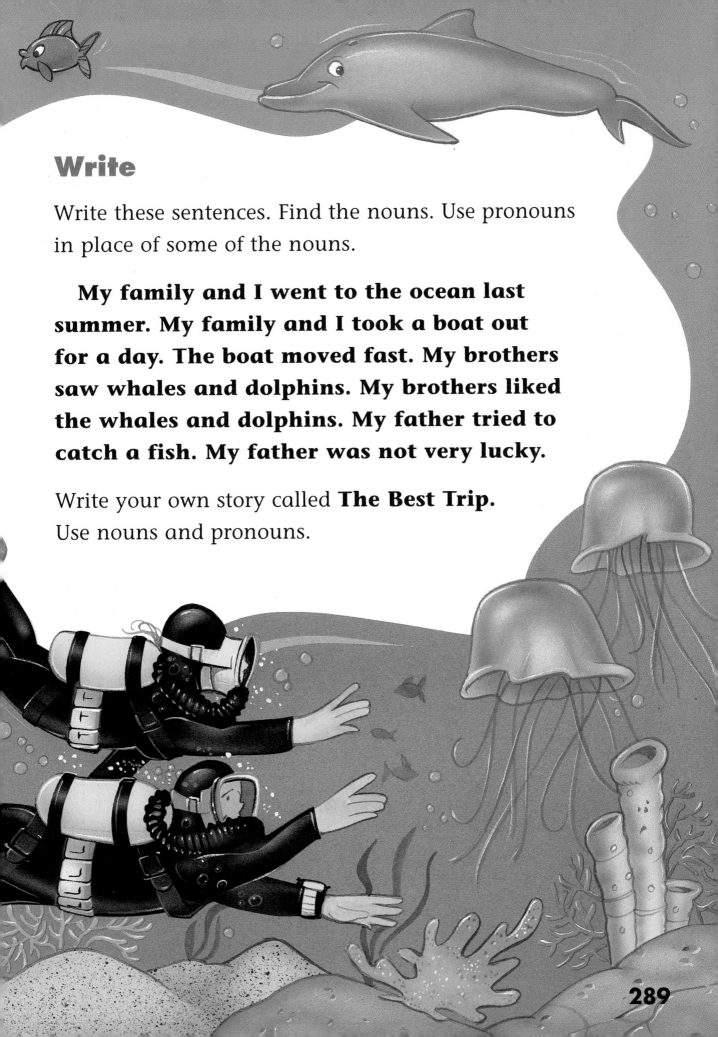

Write

Write these sentences. Find the nouns. Use pronouns in place of some of the nouns.

My family and I went to the ocean last summer. My family and I took a boat out for a day. The boat moved fast. My brothers saw whales and dolphins. My brothers liked the whales and dolphins. My father tried to catch a fish. My father was not very lucky.

Write your own story called **The Best Trip.**
Use nouns and pronouns.

Tex and the
Big Bad T. Rex

by Mary Blount Christian
illustrated by Bernard Adnet

Tex, the little dinosaur, was excited. "Mama, please read the ending again!" he said.

Mama reread, "Big Bad T. Rex said, 'I will probably eat you right now!' But Little Green Tail said, 'Not this day,' and she ran away fast."

Tex said, "If T. Rex comes along someday, I will scare him away like this." He yelled, *"Gleep!"*

Lexie, his big sister, giggled. "Oh, I am so scared," she teased.

"Be kind to your brother!" Mama exclaimed. "It is unfair to tease him."

Then Mama explained, "You are very brave, Tex, but Big Bad T. Rex goes *GRRRONK!* It would probably be better for you to run and disappear right away."

The next day, Tex and Lexie were exploring an unusual trail. Tex was in front.

Suddenly, Tex heard *"GRRRONK!"*

He cried, *"Gleep, gleep!"* and ran as fast as he could.

Tex saw a hollow log. He tried to hide there, but only his head would fit inside!

"Gleep, gleep!" he repeated. It came out the other end sounding more like *"GRRRRRONK!"*

The noise scared Lexie. She ran along the trail as fast as she could back to Mama.

"*Gleep, gleep!*" she cried.

Tex said to himself. "Someday, when I am big, I expect to have an extremely big voice. For now, I will keep my noisy log."

The next day, Tex and Lexie were again on the trail. Suddenly, there was Big Bad T. Rex right in front of them! T. Rex began chasing Lexie!

Tex stuck his head in his log. He yelled with all his might, *"Gleep!"* That *gleep* traveled through the log. It came out *"GRRRRRONK!"*

The noise was so loud that T. Rex ran. He disappeared fast.

"Tex!" Lexie exclaimed. "You are braver than Little Green Tail!"

Tex smiled. He knew that all along.

LET'S GO DINOSAUR TRACKING!

by Miriam Schlein
illustrated by Phil Wilson

Put on your boots. Put on your pith helmet. And take some water in a canteen. We're going to do some dinosaur tracking.

Here's the first set of tracks. Who made them, and what do they tell us?

We know one thing right away. Each footprint is 38 inches long. Whoever made these tracks sure was big. And heavy!

Look how deep the footprints are. We can stand in them. There's a fish swimming in one! Who made these giant steps?

More than 100 million years ago a big sauropod walked by along a mud flat by the side of a lagoon. The feet that made these footprints probably carried a 70-foot-long body that might have weighed 30 tons. No wonder they sank so deep in the mud!

Sand blew over the mud and covered the tracks. In time—millions and millions of years of time—the mud turned to stone and saved these tracks to tell us that all those years ago a sauropod went by here.

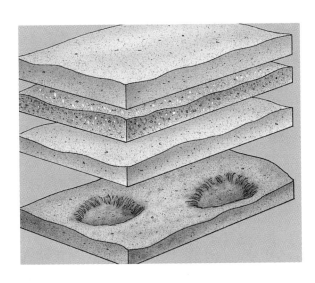

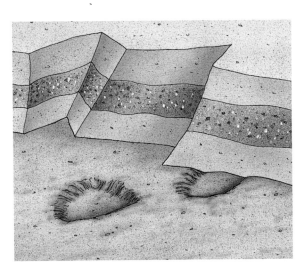

Look! The sauropod wasn't alone.
Here are different tracks—with three
pointy claws.

These are probably the footprints of an allosaur—a meat-eater, with big jaws and sharp, curved teeth.

Spying the sauropod, the allosaur began running after it. The sauropod looked like a good meal.

Did the big sauropod get away?

We don't know. The tracks lead under a big limestone cliff. We can't get to them.

Maybe someday we'll find out how the story ended.

These chase tracks were discovered near the town of Glen Rose, Texas, in 1938, by dinosaur expert Roland Bird. People around there always thought they were just big holes in the ground. But when Bird saw them, he knew right away they were dino tracks, probably the tracks of a sauropod.

Another time when Roland Bird was in Texas, someone said to him, "Say, do you want to see some elephant tracks?"

Bird went with the man to a ranch near San Antonio.

The tracks were formed more than 100 million years ago. There were no elephants then!

So—who made these "elephant tracks"?

The truth is, it was another sauropod. The tracks look different from the others because these are only the front footprints.

Now wait a minute! Was the sauropod doing some kind of balancing act, walking on its front feet?

What was going on, anyhow?

Here's a clue. Have you ever pushed yourself along in shallow water, "walking" on your hands along the bottom? Your body and feet drift behind you.

That's what the sauropod was doing—pushing itself along in water with its front feet, leaving these "elephant tracks."

Let's go! There are other tracks to follow! Here we are, in a limestone quarry. What's this? Chicken tracks? What's a chicken doing back in dinosaur times?

It does look like chicken tracks. But you're right. There were no chickens in dinosaur times. The tracks were made by a chicken-sized dinosaur named compsognathus.

One hundred forty-five million years ago this 2-foot-long, 6-pound mini-dino ran along on skinny legs and birdlike feet.

What was it doing? It was probably chasing a little lizard, which it ate. The compsognathus is one of the smallest dinosaurs we know of.

Well, this pith helmet is hot.
My canteen is empty. My boots are
covered with mud.

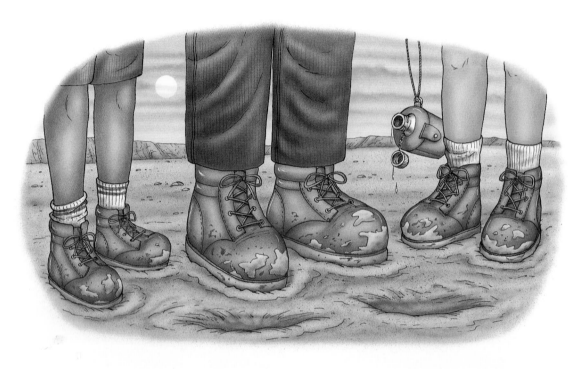

Let's go home and think about the things we've learned from tracking dinosaurs.

About the Author and Illustrator

Miriam Schlein

Miriam Schlein has been writing children's books for over forty years. She enjoys writing about animals. In addition to *Let's Go Dinosaur Tracking!* she has written several other books about dinosaurs.

Phil Wilson

Phil Wilson has been fascinated with dinosaurs since he was very young. His mother still has crayon drawings of dinosaurs he drew when he was in third grade.

Mr. Wilson has a large library of dinosaur books. He always does research to make sure that the dinosaurs and the landscape he is drawing are correct.

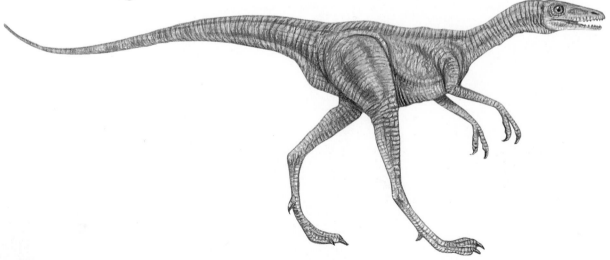

Strange Footprints

by Vivian Gouled

It seemed that a giant
Tramped through the snow,
Or maybe an elephant—
No one could know.

Everyone guessed
Whose the footprints could be,
But no one imagined
Galoshes and me!

Reader Response

Let's Talk

Now that you have read the story, are you more interested in dinosaurs? Why or why not?

Let's Think

What would someone need to know before going dinosaur tracking?

Test Prep
Let's Write

How are dinosaur tracks formed? Look back and read to find the answer. Write sentences to explain.

Make a Dinosaur Footprint

The children in the story find a dinosaur track that is 38 inches long. Make your own dinosaur footprint.

1. Use a large sheet of paper.
2. Use a ruler to measure inches. Measure 38 inches.
3. Draw a dinosaur footprint.
4. How many classmates' shoes can fit in the footprint? Write your answer.

Language Arts

Contractions

A **contraction** is a short way to put two words together. An apostrophe **'** takes the place of one or more letters.

You can make a contraction by putting together a verb and the word **not.**

is + not = isn't
The dinosaur **is not** small.
The dinosaur **isn't** small.

You can also make a contraction by putting a pronoun together with words like **will, are, am, have,** or **is.**

I + will = I'll
I will draw a picture.
I'll draw a picture.

they + are = they're
They are looking at a *T. rex*.
They're looking at a *T. rex*.

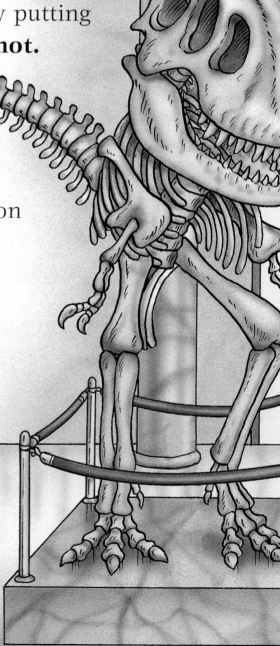

Talk

Make up sentences about the picture.
Use contractions from the list below.

contractions					
I'll	he's	they're	don't	she's	I'm
can't	she'll	we're	you're	isn't	we'll

Write

Write these sentences. Choose the correct contraction.

1. <u>We will</u> write a dinosaur report.
(We'll, She'll)

2. <u>He is</u> drawing the picture. (She's, He's)

3. I <u>do not</u> like to draw. (don't, can't)

4. <u>I will </u>write the dinosaur facts. (We'll, I'll)

Write your own sentences about dinosaurs. Use contractions.

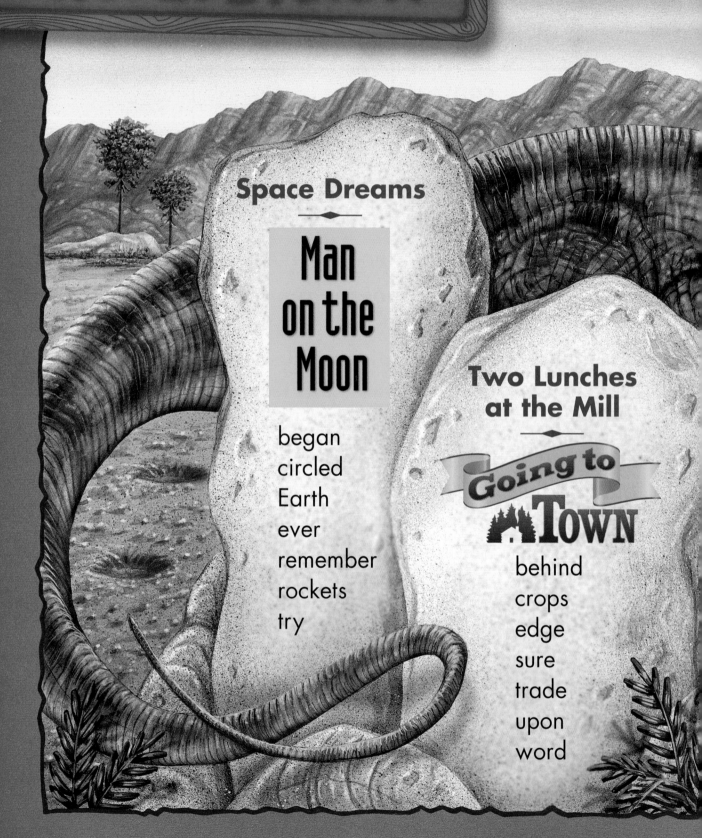

Space Dreams

Man on the Moon

began
circled
Earth
ever
remember
rockets
try

Two Lunches
at the Mill

Going to
TOWN

behind
crops
edge
sure
trade
upon
word

A True
Boating Family

—◆—

Riding the Ferry
with Captain Cruz

course
deck
dock
steers
things
years

Tex and the Big
Bad T. Rex

—◆—

LET'S GO
DINOSAUR TRACKING!

claws
front
giant
helmet
probably
someday
stone

Splash

—◆—

Down in the Sea:
The
Jellyfish

beach
floating
flopped
grow
near
poke

Test Talk

Use Information from the Story

The answer to a question may be in the story. You will have to look back in the story to find the answer.

Read this paragraph and question about *Going to Town.*

They walked up to the biggest building in town. This was the store where Pa came to trade. As they climbed up the steps of the store, Laura was so excited that she was trembling all over.

1. How does Laura feel when she walks up the steps of the store?

A tired

B angry

C excited

Find words in the paragraph from the story that answer the question.

Here is how one girl chose her answer.

The question asks how Laura felt. The last sentence in the paragraph says that she was excited and trembling. That must be the answer.

Try it!

Use what you have learned to answer this question about *Going to Town*. Look at page 219 to find words to answer the question.

2. Why hadn't Mary or Laura ever been to town?

Ⓐ **They had to help their mother.**

Ⓑ **They were too young.**

Ⓒ **They had to go to bed.**

Just ★ Imagine!

How do we use
our imaginations
to do things?

The Clubhouse

by Anne Phillips
illustrated by Rosario Valderrama

Rosie found a box. It was big enough for a clubhouse.

"I believe it needs flowers," Rosie said to herself. She got some paint. She painted a few flowers on the box. She painted a few more.

"What are you doing?" asked her big brother, Tomás.

"Making a clubhouse," said Rosie.

"It needs a door," said Tomás.

Tomás got some scissors. He cut out a door. Rosie kept painting. She painted a number above the door.

Tomás cut out another piece. It was a window. It looked like half a moon.

"What are you doing?" asked Annie.

"We are making a clubhouse," said Rosie and Tomás.

"It needs curtains," said Annie.

Annie got a piece of cloth. It was big enough to make a curtain. Annie glued it above the window. Then she painted a keyhole.

Rosie painted a doorknob halfway up the door.

Tomás cut out another window.

"What are you doing?" asked Stanley.

"We are making a clubhouse," said Rosie and Tomás and Annie.

"It needs chairs," said Stanley.

Stanley found some boxes. The boxes made good chairs. Rosie painted *CLUBHOUSE* above the window. Annie glued a curtain above another window. Tomás hung a photograph of himself inside.

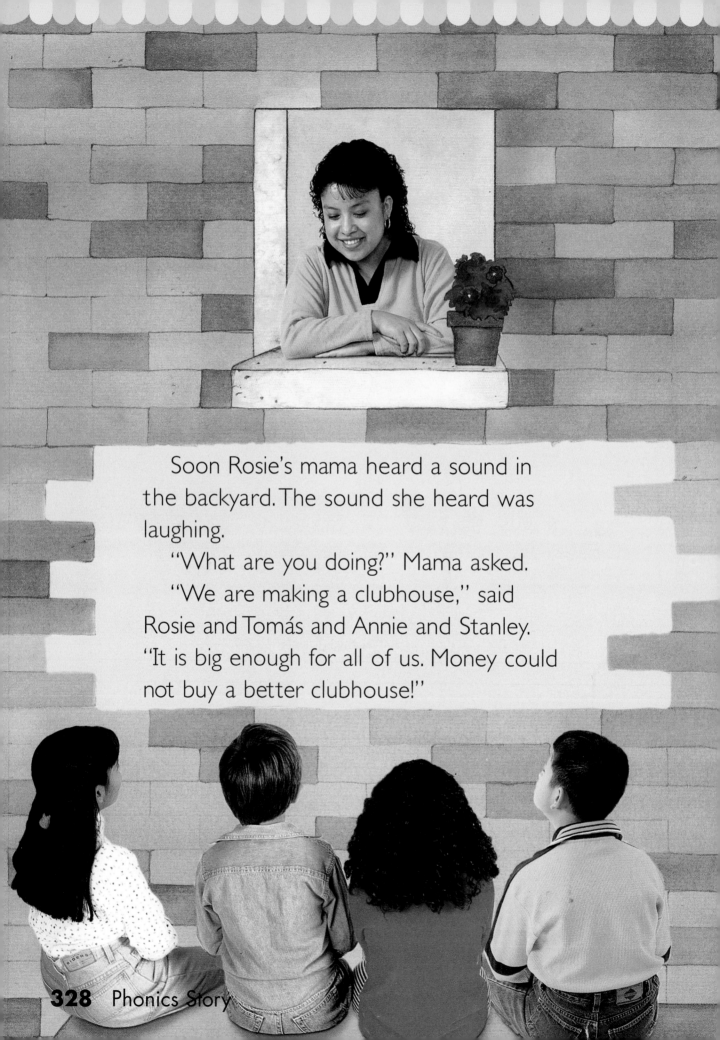

Soon Rosie's mama heard a sound in the backyard. The sound she heard was laughing.

"What are you doing?" Mama asked.

"We are making a clubhouse," said Rosie and Tomás and Annie and Stanley. "It is big enough for all of us. Money could not buy a better clubhouse!"

"I believe it needs one more thing," said Mama.
She got a plate of cookies. They were warm and
smelled like honey.

"What a relief! Now our clubhouse is just right,"
said Rosie and Tomás and Annie and Stanley.

And it was.

Lemonade for Sale

by Stuart J. Murphy

illustrated by Tricia Tusa

The members of the Elm Street Kids'
Club were feeling glum.

"Our clubhouse is falling down,
and our piggybank is empty," Meg said.

"I know how we can make some
money," said Matthew. "Let's sell
lemonade."

Danny said, "I bet if we can sell about
30 or 40 cups each day for a week, we'll
make enough money to fix our
clubhouse. Let's keep track of our sales."

Sheri said, "I can make a bar graph. I'll
list the number of cups up the side like
this. I'll show the days of the week along
the bottom like this."

On Monday they set up their corner stand. When people walked by, Petey, Meg's pet parrot, squawked, "Lemonade for sale! Lemonade for sale!"

Matthew squeezed the lemons.

Meg mixed in some sugar.

Danny shook it up with ice and poured it into cups.

Sheri kept track of how many cups they sold.

Sheri announced, "We sold 30 cups today. I'll fill in the bar above Monday up to the 30 on the side."

"Not bad," said Danny.

"Not bad. Not bad," chattered Petey.

On Tuesday Petey squawked again,
"Lemonade for sale! Lemonade for sale!"
and more people came by.

Matthew squeezed more lemons.

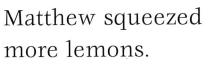

Meg mixed in more sugar.

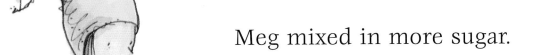

Danny shook it up with ice and poured it into more cups.

Sheri kept track of how many cups they sold.

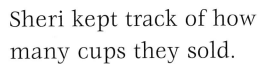

Sheri shouted, "We sold 40 cups today. I'll fill in the bar above Tuesday up to the number 40. The bars show that our sales are going up."

"Things are looking good," said Meg.

"Looking good. Looking good," chattered Petey.

On Wednesday Petey squawked,
"Lemonade for sale!" so many times that
most of the neighborhood stopped by.

Matthew squeezed
even more lemons.

Meg mixed in even more sugar.

Danny shook it up with
ice and poured it into
even more cups.

Sheri kept track of how
many cups they sold.

Sheri yelled, "We sold 56 cups today. I'll fill in Wednesday's bar up to a little more than halfway between 50 and 60."

"That's great," shouted Matthew.

"That's great! That's great!" bragged Petey.

They opened again on Thursday, but something was wrong. No matter how many times Petey squawked, "Lemonade for sale!" hardly anyone stopped by.

Matthew squeezed just
a few lemons.

Meg mixed in only
a couple of spoonfuls
of sugar.

Danny's ice melted
while he waited.

Sheri kept track of the few
cups that they sold.

Sheri said, "We sold only 24 cups today.
Thursday's bar is way down low."
"There goes our clubhouse," said Danny sadly.
Petey didn't make a sound.

"I think I know what's going on," said Matthew. "Look!" He pointed down the street. "There's someone juggling on that corner, and everyone's going over there to watch."

"Let's check it out," said Meg.
Danny asked the juggler, "Who are you?"
"I'm Jed," said the juggler. "I just moved here."

Sheri had an idea. She whispered
something to Jed.

On Friday, Sheri arrived with Jed.

"Jed's going to juggle right next to our stand," Sheri said.

That day Petey squawked, Jed juggled, and more people came by than ever before.

Matthew squeezed
loads of lemons.

Meg mixed in
tons of sugar.

Danny shook it up with lots of
ice and almost ran out of cups.

Sheri could hardly keep track
of how many cups they sold.

"We sold so many cups today that our sales are over the top. We have enough money to rebuild our clubhouse."

"Hooray!" they all shouted. "Jed! Jed!
Will you join our club?"

"You bet!" said Jed.

"You bet! You bet!" squawked Petey.

Bar Graph

If Friday lemonade sales for the Elm Street Kids' Club had gone to the top of the bar graph, how many cups of lemonade would that be? Look at the graph below to see.

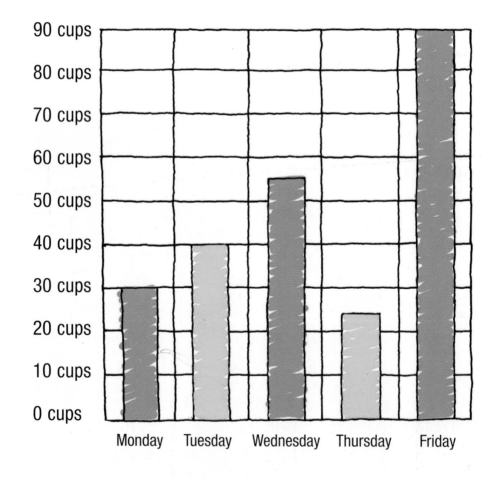

Circle Graph

If Sheri had kept track of the lemonade sales on a circle graph instead of a bar graph, it might have looked like this one.

How many cups of lemonade were sold on Monday?

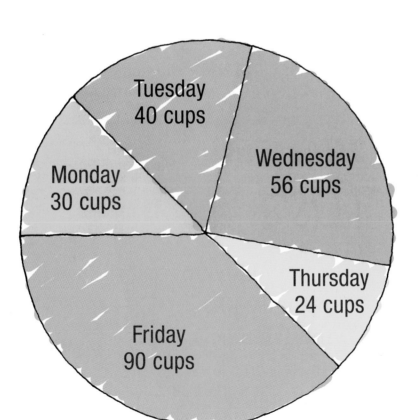

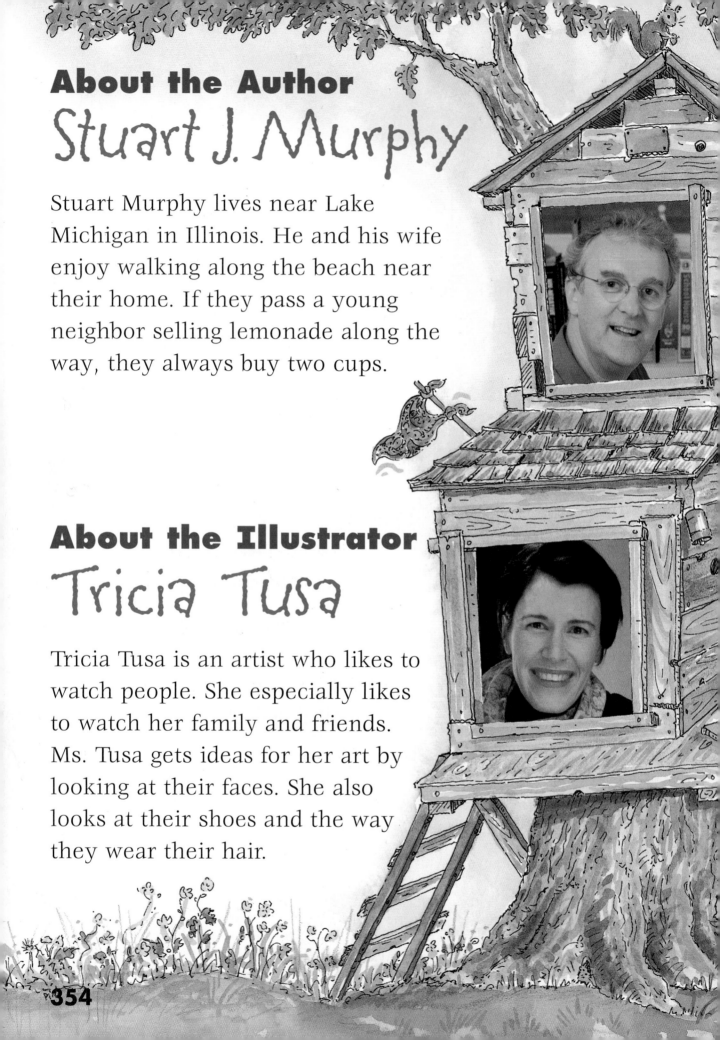

About the Author
Stuart J. Murphy

Stuart Murphy lives near Lake Michigan in Illinois. He and his wife enjoy walking along the beach near their home. If they pass a young neighbor selling lemonade along the way, they always buy two cups.

About the Illustrator
Tricia Tusa

Tricia Tusa is an artist who likes to watch people. She especially likes to watch her family and friends. Ms. Tusa gets ideas for her art by looking at their faces. She also looks at their shoes and the way they wear their hair.

Lemonade
for Sale

by John Ciardi

Cut the lemon through the peel.
   The juice is all inside.
When you squeeze it (if it squirts)
   You must step aside.

Lemon squirt can make you smart
   If it hits your eye.
Well, it might not work for you.
   You won't know till you try.

Sugar in the sugar tin.
   Water in the tap.
Fill the pitcher to the brim.
   Hold it in your lap.

When it's full enough you'll feel
   Water down your shin.
That's the time to put a hundred
   Ice cubes in.

Reader Response

Let's Talk

If you had a
lemonade sale,
how would you get
people to come?

Let's Think

The children use a bar
graph in the story.
How did it help them?

Test Prep
Let's Write

Write a news story about
the children's lemonade
sale. Give your story a
headline. Read your story
to the class.

Lemonade
TIMES
Big Sales
at Lemonade Stand!

Lemonade

Make a Poster

Pretend you are having a lemonade sale. Make a poster telling about your sale.

1. Draw an interesting picture that will make people stop and buy your lemonade.
2. Write what you plan to do with the money.
3. Show how much each cup of lemonade will cost.
4. Compare your poster with a classmate's poster.

Language Arts

Sentences

A **sentence** is a group of words that tells a complete idea. There are four kinds of sentences: **statement, command, question,** and **exclamation.** Begin every sentence with a capital letter.

Put a **.** at the end of a statement and a command.
The car wash is today.
Wash each window carefully.

Put a **?** at the end of a question.
How much does it cost?

Put an **!** at the end of an exclamation.
The dog is getting us wet!

Talk

Tell a story about the picture. Take turns adding sentences to the story. Use the four kinds of sentences.

Grant School Car Wash $2.00

Write

Write each sentence correctly. Use a capital letter and the correct ending mark.

1. this car wash is so much fun
2. pay the man in the booth
3. the car was dirty
4. who forgot to tie up the dog

Write sentences to answer the questions below. Use different kinds of sentences.

What job would you like to do to make money? Why? How would it make you feel?

Start Collecting! It's Fun!

by Joanne Ryder

Shells, dolls, leaves, rocks . . .

Stamps, coins, trains, clocks . . .

People collect all sorts of things! Maybe you would like to start collecting something too. It can be a great hobby for a young person.

Off to a Good Start

Many collections are easy to start. But it's good to learn more about the things you collect. You can either read books or ask people for help.

Now let's meet some young people who collect things. They'll tell you something about themselves as you read what they like to collect.

Look in Your Own Backyard

You don't have to go far to find things to collect. Start by looking around you. That is how Neil began to collect leaves.

"I found these gingko leaves by the road," said Neil.

"Leaves have great shapes," he told us. "They can either be long, round, or shaped like hands. I like to collect them all."

A Beary Nice Gift

You might start to collect something you receive as a gift.

"I received my first bear eight years ago," said Sheila. "Sassy is still my favorite, but now I have twenty-eight bears that sit on shelves in my bedroom.

"My sister and I like to dress the bears," she said. "We make capes and scarves for them to wear."

A House Full of Hats

"I collect hats," said Jake. "I like funny hats, tall hats, and round hats.

"I receive hats as gifts, either for my birthday or as a surprise," Jake added. "I hang my hats all over the house. I even hang them from the ceiling!

"Once I found a hat on the side of a road," said Jake. "Someone didn't want it, but I did."

Start Collecting!

Choosing a collection is like choosing a friend. Pick one that is good for you.

"Collect what you love," said Sheila. "I love bears, and I love finding new ones."

It is fun to collect. Start now, while you are young, and watch your collection grow and grow.

The Puddle Pail

by Elisa Kleven

One bright morning after a storm, Ernst, a young blue crocodile, and his big green brother, Sol, set off for the beach. They skipped through the wet grass and stamped through the mud, drumming on their shiny pails.

"I'm going to fill my pail with shells," said Sol, who loved to collect things.

"I'm going to fill my pail with sand and build a sand castle," said Ernst, who loved to make things.

"Maybe I'll find some rocks too," said Sol, "all shapes and colors, for my rock collection. And some feathers, for my feather collection, and maybe some string." Sol bent down to pick up a rubber band. "Just the thing for my rubber band collection! You ought to start a collection, Ernst."

"I don't know what to collect," Ernst replied.

"Collect something you really like," said Sol. "Something that comes in all different sizes and colors and shapes. That way your collection will be interesting."

Ernst watched the clouds make flower shapes and sea horse shapes in the windy sky. He watched a little snake cloud puff up into a dragon. He watched a rabbit cloud curl into a ball.

"Clouds are interesting," he said. "I wish I could collect clouds."

"Clouds!" exclaimed Sol. "You can't collect clouds! Think of something else you like."

"Stars," said Ernst, imagining the sky at night. "I love to watch the stars."

"But you can't collect stars, either," said Sol. They're too far away and too big and very, very hot."

"They look so small and cold," said Ernst. "I wish I could collect stars."

"I know!" said Sol. "Starfishes! You could collect *them.*"

"I like starfishes in the ocean," said Ernst. "But I don't think I want to collect them."

"Well," Sol suggested, "what about star-shaped cookies? You could collect star-shaped butter cookies with frosting—"

"And star-shaped chocolate cookies with sprinkles," Ernst added.

"And star-shaped cherry cookies with toasted nuts!" said Sol.

Ernst's mouth watered. "I wish I could collect a bunch of cookies right now—in my stomach!"

Just then, something caught Sol's eye—a bottle cap lying in a puddle. "Look at that sparkly bottle cap, Ernst. You could start a bottle cap collection!"

"It's pretty," Ernst agreed. "But I like the puddle it's in even more."

"The puddle?" said Sol.

"It looks like a little piece of sky on the ground. I wish I could collect *it*."

"You can't collect puddles," said Sol.

"Yes, I can collect puddles," said Ernst. "They're not too far away or too big or too hot—and I don't want to eat them." *Splish-splash,* Ernst scooped the puddle into his pail.

"Ernst," said Sol, "you're not really going to start a puddle collection, are you?"

"Yes," said Ernst. "I am." He scooped up a green puddle, round as a saucer. *Splash-splosh,* it joined the other puddle in the pail.

Sol rolled his eyes. "Since you're going to stay here collecting puddles, I'll go down to the beach by myself and collect *real* things."

Puddles are real, thought Ernst, as he searched for more to collect. "Here's a purple puddle . . .

and a striped one

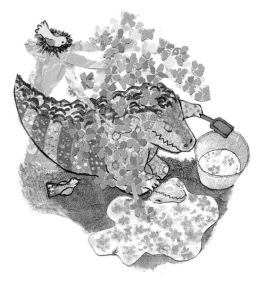

and a flowered one.

Here's a puddle full of diamonds and a puddle full of squares . . .

a puddle full of gumballs and a puddle full of brooms, a puddle like an Easter egg,

a puddle like a wheel, and a puddle with a pretzel in it.

Slippery puddles, smooth puddles, lemony, lettery cool puddles." Ernst sang a song as he scooped the puddles up. *Splish-splash* sang the puddles as they slid into the pail.

Sol came back with his pail piled high. "Look what I got, Ernst! Twelve seashells,

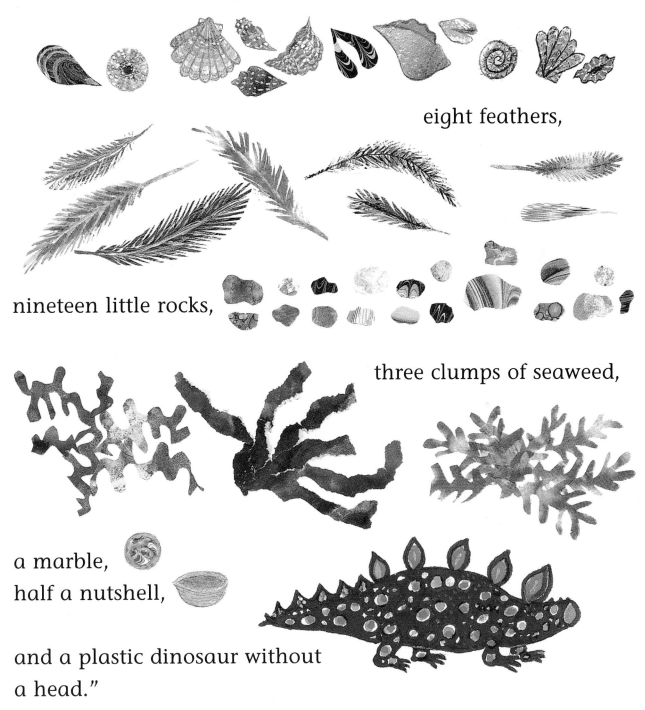

eight feathers,

nineteen little rocks,

three clumps of seaweed,

a marble,
half a nutshell,

and a plastic dinosaur without
a head."

"I got a lot of puddles," Ernst announced. "All different sizes and colors and shapes."

Sol peered into Ernst's pail. "Your puddles have all run together! They look like a pail full of ordinary water!"

"They're one *big* puddle now," said Ernst. "An Ernst and Sol puddle!"

"That's the weirdest collection I've ever heard of," Sol replied. "What can you do with a puddle?"

"I'll think of something." Ernst carried his pail carefully as they started for home.

"I know!" said Sol. "You can help me wash the sand off all my new collections."

"You can wash your own collections," Ernst replied. "I'll think of something else to do with my puddle."

Ernst set his puddle pail on the grass and sat down to swing. While he swung, his puddle slowly turned from gold to pink. Clouds swam in and out of it like fishes.

When night fell, stars collected in the puddle pail—and a little piece of the moon too.

Early the next morning, Ernst went out to check on his pail. A thirsty dog was drinking from it. "You like my magic puddle soup?" Ernst asked. The dog wagged her tail and drank some more, leaving Ernst just enough water to paint some watercolor pictures.

Ernst painted the dog,

and he painted some clouds

and some stars and many puddles.

Sol came by, his pail filled with flowers and acorns and leaves. "I started some new collections," he said. "What have you got there, Ernst?"

"A dog," replied Ernst. "And a painting collection."

"Oooh!" said Sol. "What a collection! With clouds and stars and everything."

"I used part of my puddle collection to make it," Ernst explained. "The dog drank the other part."

Ernst petted the dog. He looked at the clouds and the stars and the puddles shining on the grass. He felt proud and happy—and hungry too, since he hadn't eaten breakfast yet.

"Let's go collect blackberries," he said, "from the bushes down the road."

"Good idea!" Sol grabbed his pail. "Maybe we'll find some pennies on the way, and some pinecones and gum wrappers."

"And maybe some shadows too," said Ernst.

"Shadows!" said Sol. "You can't—"

"Yes, I can collect shadows!" Ernst cried. He caught one for a second in his pail.

And when it fluttered off, he and Sol filled their pails—and themselves—with sweet, juicy blackberries.

About the Author/Illustrator
Elisa Kleven

Elisa Kleven enjoys collecting things, just like her characters Ernst and Sol.

Ms. Kleven places real objects, such as lace and wool, into her artwork. She likes to "experiment, arrange, rearrange, and discover joyful surprises" as she works. "I love to snip and glue scraps of this and that into new shapes," she says.

Creating her characters reminds Ms. Kleven of playing with toys!

Reader Response

Let's Talk

If you could collect anything from the story, what would you collect?

Let's Think

Why does Ernst think he is collecting clouds, stars, and a piece of the moon in his puddle pail?

Test Prep
Let's Write

Do you like to collect things like Sol, or do you like to make things like Ernst? Choose one character to write a letter to. Tell him what you like to do.

Make a Puddle Pail

Ernst says he collects clouds, stars, and a
piece of the moon with his puddle pail.
He also paints pictures. What can
you do with a puddle pail?

1. Find a pail and fill it with water.
2. Place the pail under a light.
3. Hold objects above the pail.
    Tell friends what you see.
4. Add food coloring to a cup of the water.
    Paint a picture. Share it with classmates.

Language Arts

Quotation Marks

Quotation marks " " show the beginning and end of what someone says.

Miles asked, "What is your favorite stamp?" "This one," said Billy.

Talk

Tell a classmate what the children in the pictures might say about their collections. When someone is speaking, hold up your fingers in the shape of quotation marks.

Write

Write the sentences correctly. Put " at the beginning of what someone says. Put " at the end of what someone says.

1. Jenny said, Look I found a button on the floor.

2. My beads are beautiful! Mia exclaimed.

Write a story with two characters. Have the characters talk about things they like to collect. Use quotation marks.

Stone Soup

a folktale retold by Lily Toy Hong

One day a peddler crossed a bridge into a town. He stopped his wagon and sat down on a rock. The peddler was hungry. He asked a fair lady if she had any spare food.

"I don't mean to be unkind," she said, "but we don't have food for ourselves."

The peddler took a big black pot from his wagon. "I can make stone soup for us to share."

The lady just stared. "Stone soup?"

"You'll see," said the peddler. "First I need water."

The lady got some water. The peddler filled the pot and lit a fire.

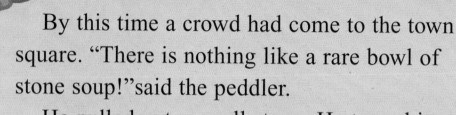

By this time a crowd had come to the town square. "There is nothing like a rare bowl of stone soup!"said the peddler.

He pulled out a small stone. He tossed it over the edge of the pot. "Now we wait," said the peddler.

"Wait if you dare," said the butcher. "But you'll never get soup."

The peddler stirred and sniffed the air. "This soup I'm making will be fine," he said. "But it would taste even better with beets."
A woman stepped up to the edge of the pot. She held up a pair of beets. She said, "Add these to the soup, if you care to." The peddler threw them into the pot.

"This soup I'm making smells good," he said. "But it would taste even better with potatoes."

A boy with red hair said, "I found two potatoes! You can add both."

The peddler dropped in the potatoes. "If only we had a carrot," he said.

"These are from my garden," a woman said.

The peddler licked his lips. He put in the carrots. Then he said, "Onions would add flavor to this soup I'm making."

"I will share my onions," a man said. The peddler added them to the soup.

The air filled with a delicious smell. "This stone soup I'm making is good. But it would taste even better if it had some beef."

"I guess I can give you some," grumbled the butcher. He put some beef into the pot.

At last the peddler took a taste. He smiled and said, "This stone soup I am making is the best of any I have ever prepared."

"I'll be the judge of that!" shouted the butcher. He took a taste and smiled. "The peddler is right!"

The peddler dished out a fair share to everyone. They ate until there wasn't any left. That night the peddler left without a care. And long after, the people talked about the man who made soup from a stone.

Stone Soup

by The Children's Television Workshop
illustrated by Eileen Mueller Neill

Characters

Narrator	Sal Lamie	Rick Cotta
Ida Know	Vida Minn	Frank Furter
Minnie Stronie	Brock Lee	Artie Choke
Ann Chovie	Bill Lownie	

Scene One

Narrator: In the village of Bellie Acres, it was time for the annual "Souper Bowl" contest. The person who created the best soup would receive a soup ladle made of solid gold. The night before the contest, Minnie Stronie called up her best friend, Ann Chovie.

Minnie Stronie: I hope the judges like this year's batch of my famous "Minnie Stronie" soup!

Ann Chovie: Well, I've been cooking all day, and my husband told me my "Ann Chovie" soup is still way too salty!

Minnie Stronie: Did you hear who the judges are? Brock Lee and Sal Lamie. They're tough!

Ann Chovie: I suppose Ida Know will win. She's taken the Golden Ladle three years in a row!

Minnie Stronie: Oh, oh—I've got to go, Ann. My soup is boiling over.

Ann Chovie: Bye, Minnie. Good luck!

Scene Two

Narrator: It's the day of the big contest. Sal Lamie and Brock Lee are tasting the soups. They both stop for second helpings at Ida Know's bowl.

Sal Lamie: This is delicious! What do you call this wonderful soup?

Ida Know: I don't know!

Brock Lee: This soup is both sweet and sour at the same time. What's in it?

Ida Know: I don't know!

Narrator: Frank Furter was jealous.

Frank Furter: Just once I'd like to be the big wiener—
I mean *winner* at this contest!

Narrator: Vida Minn was angry.

Vida Minn: What's so great about Ida Know's soup?
Now, my soup is good for you! It has vitamins A,
B, and C!

Narrator: The judges were about to declare Ida Know
the winner—when suddenly a stranger appeared
carrying a large black soup kettle.

Stranger: Am I too late? My soup isn't ready yet—but it won't take long to prepare. And I bet it will win!

Sal Lamie: What's your name, sir, and what kind of soup will you make?

Stranger: I'm Bill. Bill Lownie. And I'm making stone soup.

Everyone: STONE SOUP?

Frank Furter: *(to Ida)* How do you make stone soup?

Ida Know: I don't know!

Narrator: Everyone watched as Bill Lownie filled his kettle with water to boil.

Bill: Now I'll just add this ordinary stone. *(He drops a large stone into the kettle. PLUNK!)*

Scene Three

Narrator: Everyone was quiet as Bill Lownie stirred his stone soup. After a little while, he tasted it.

Brock Lee: Well? Is it soup yet?

Bill: I just feel bad I didn't bring a carrot. Stone soup just isn't the same without a little chopped carrot thrown in.

Minnie Stronie: Well, I guess I can spare a carrot. *(She hands him one.)*

Bill: Oh, thank you so much! *(He adds it and stirs for a while, then tastes the soup again.)* Well it's *almost* perfect. This would be the best batch of stone soup I ever made . . . if I only had a potato.

Vida Minn: Here's a potato for you, Mr. Lownie! It's full of Vitamin C!

Bill: You are a kind lady. *(He stirs some more. The aroma of the soup begins to grow.)* Now let's see . . . You know, my mom always added a little scrap of fresh meat. I don't suppose any of you . . .

Frank Furter: *(handing Bill some meat)* Help yourself!

Bill: Now just a little salt and pepper . . .

Ann Chovie: I have those! *(She hands them to him.)*

Bill: And some garlic . . . maybe an onion.

Minnie Stronie: *(whispering)* Ask Artie Choke if he brought any garlic with him. And I think Rick Cotta has an onion.

Artie Choke: *(handing over garlic)* Good luck, pal!

Rick Cotta: Here's your onion. And I brought you a little grated cheese too.

Ann Chovie: *(sniffing)* Mmm! Doesn't the stone soup smell delicious?

Frank Furter: It sure does!

Bill: It just has to cook a little bit more.

Narrator: Finally, Sal Lamie and Brock Lee tasted the stone soup.

Sal Lamie: This is magnificent!

Brock Lee: We declare Bill Lownie the winner with his amazing stone soup!

Everyone: Yay!

Bill Lownie: Thanks. I'm in a hurry, so I'll just take my Golden Ladle and be on my way. *(He leaves.)*

Artie Choke: How did he ever make such great soup out of a stone?

Ida Know: I don't know!

Minnie Stronie: I want the recipe!

Ann Chovie: Imagine, all you need is a stone!

Frank Furter: *(thinking)* And a carrot, and a potato, and some meat . . . . Hey Bill Lownie! Come back here!! Somebody catch him!!!

The End

About the Illustrator
Eileen Mueller Neill

Before Eileen Mueller Neill begins to make her clay creations, she draws. "My drawings come to life in clay," says Ms. Neill. "There is something magical about it."

Ms. Neill uses tools to shape the colorful clay into shapes. Then she bakes them carefully so that they become hard. She then glues them onto a board. She often paints the pieces to get the right color. Sometimes she adds fabric, paper, or wood for just the right look.

Spaghetti! Spaghetti!

by Jack Prelutsky
illustrated by
Nancy Freeman

Spaghetti! spaghetti!
you're wonderful stuff,
I love you, spaghetti,
I can't get enough.
You're covered with sauce
and you're sprinkled with cheese,
spaghetti! spaghetti!
oh, give me some please.

Spaghetti! spaghetti!
piled high in a mound,
you wiggle, you wriggle,
you squiggle around.
There's slurpy spaghetti
all over my plate,
spaghetti! spaghetti!
I think you are great.

Spaghetti! spaghetti!
I love you a lot,
you're slishy, you're sloshy,
delicious and hot.
I gobble you down
oh, I can't get enough,
spaghetti! spaghetti!
you're wonderful stuff.

Reader Response

Let's Talk

Would you want Bill Lownie to be your friend? Why or why not?

Let's Think

Who really made the stone soup? Explain.

Test Prep
Let's Write

Write your own special soup recipe. Make a list of all the things you want to put in your soup. Then tell how to make it.

Make Costumes

The characters in the play have tricky names.
Make a costume to go with one character's name.

1. Choose one character. Think of a costume that fits that character's name.

2. Get what you need. Make a costume for your character.

3. Read the play with classmates. Wear your costume as you read your character's part.

Language Arts

Commas

A **comma** looks like this **,** . You use commas often when you write.

Use commas to separate three or more words in a list.

Lisa made soup with corn, carrots, and potatoes.

Use a comma between the day of the week, the date, and the year.

Lisa went to cooking class on Saturday, May 14, 20_ _.

Use a comma after the greeting and closing in a letter.

Dear Uncle Joe,   **Love,**
                                        Lisa

                             May 16, 20_ _

Dear Uncle Joe,

    Bill and I went to a cooking class last Saturday, May 14. We made soup with carrots, corn, and potatoes. It was fun!

                     Love,
                     Lisa

Talk

Look in stories you have read. Find commas in lists, dates, and letters. Tell why the comma is there.

Write

Copy this letter. Add the missing commas.

April 12 20_ _

Dear Grandma

   We're having a surprise party for Mom on Saturday May 3. There will be cake ice cream and presents. Please come.

Love
Dianne

Write a letter inviting a friend to dinner. Tell your friend to come on a certain day and date. Name different foods you will serve.

A Good Idea

by Diane Hoyt-Goldsmith
photographed by Nita Winter

Where do people get ideas?
A good idea can come
from just about anywhere.
Richie Stachowski and
his dad were on vacation.
They were swimming in
the ocean. Richie tried
floating on his stomach.
He watched a group of fish
swim beside him.

Then Richie saw a school of giant fish. He wanted his father to see it also. So he tried to tell his dad. But Richie was behind his dad, so his dad wasn't able to see him.

Soon Richie got an idea. "I wish I had an underwater walkie-talkie for the ocean," he thought. "Then I would be able to call my dad."

Most people would soon forget about their idea. Not Richie though! He began to read. He tried to find out how sound waves move through water. He also remembered what he learned in his science group in school.

Soon Richie began making a plastic walkie-talkie. He tried his invention over and over in a swimming pool. It worked!

Richie wanted to be able to sell his walkie-talkie in stores though, so his parents began to help.

Soon Richie's invention was in toy stores all over the United States. It was also in six other countries. His walkie-talkies are called "Water Talkies."

Richie has a busy schedule. He is now working on a new group of ideas. He is making pool toys.

Though Richie is only thirteen years old, he has his own company. It is called Short Stack Products. Richie named his company after his favorite food—a short stack of pancakes!

Maybe one day soon you will also get a good idea. Who knows what you'll be able to do with it!

Annie's Gifts

by Angela Shelf Medearis
illustrated by Anna Rich

Once there lived a family that loved music. Every morning the children, Lee, Patty, and Annie, turned on some music. The floors trembled as they stomped their feet to the loud bass beat. Soon they were moving down the street to catch the school bus.

After the children left for school, Momma would
turn on the radio. Momma swayed with the sweet
rhythm as she sipped her coffee.

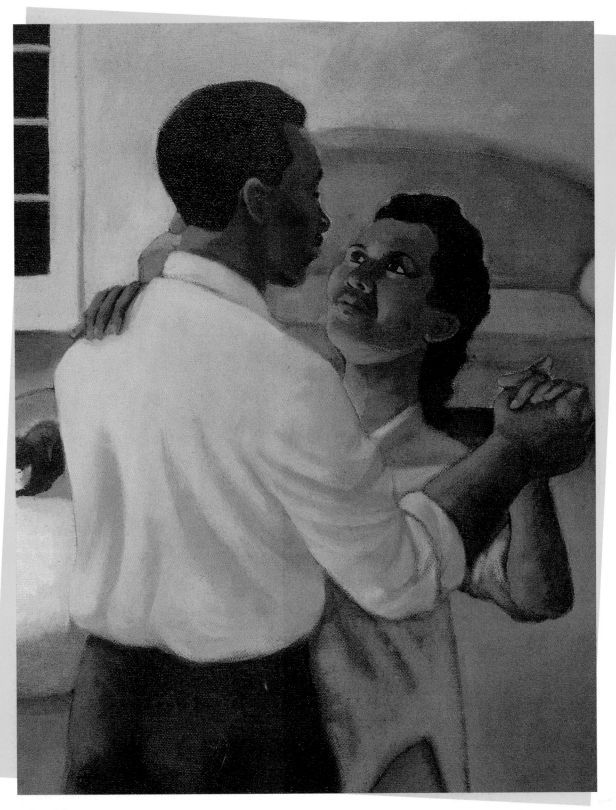

Every night, after the children were in bed, Daddy would say, "Come on, honey! Let's go once around the floor." Then he and Momma slow danced to the soulful, blues music he loved.

Lee loved music so much that he joined his school band. Annie thought Lee looked wonderful in his uniform with the shiny brass buttons. Lee's music sounded like the circus. When he swung into a song on the trumpet, Annie tapped her feet and clapped her hands.

Patty was a wonderful musician too. When Patty played the piano it made Annie think of pretty colors, soft rain, and springtime flowers. Patty also had a lovely singing voice. When company came, she would entertain the guests.

"Wonderful, just wonderful," the guests would sigh and clap their hands after Patty's performance. Annie decided that she wanted to play an instrument too.

One day, Annie's school music teacher, Mrs. Mason, passed out instruments to the class. She gave Annie a recorder.

The class practiced a group song for months. Everyone played their part perfectly, everyone, except Annie. When Annie played, the recorder squeaked and squawked like chickens at feeding time.

"I don't think the recorder is the instrument for you," Mrs. Mason said.

"I guess you're right," Annie said. "Maybe I can play the cello."

"Let's give it a try," Mrs. Mason said. "I'll show you how to play it."

When Mrs. Mason played the cello, it sounded warm and carefree, like carousel music. Annie tried and tried, but when she played the cello, it always sounded like a chorus of screeching alley cats.

"Oh," Mrs. Mason sighed and rubbed her ears. "Annie, darling, I just don't think this is the instrument for you. How would you like to make a banner and some posters announcing our program?"

"Okay," said Annie. She was disappointed, but she did love to draw. Annie drew while everyone else practiced.

That evening, Annie picked up Lee's trumpet and tried to play it. Her playing sounded like an elephant with a bad cold. Lee begged her to stop. Annie's feelings were hurt, but she put the trumpet away.

"I wish I could find an instrument to play," Annie told her mother.

"Cheer up!" Momma said. "We're going to get a new piano and everyone is going to take piano lessons!"

Soon, a beautiful, new piano was delivered to Annie's house. The piano was made of shiny, brown mahogany. Annie peeked under the piano lid while Patty played a song. "Melody Maker" was written in beautiful gold letters.

That week, all three children started piano lessons with Mrs. Kelly. After every lesson, Mrs. Kelly gave them new sheet music to practice.

Patty and Lee did very well. Mrs. Kelly always told them how talented they were.

Oh, but when Annie played the piano, Mrs. Kelly's smile turned into a frown. The low notes sounded like a diesel truck honking its horn, the middle ones like croaking frogs, and the high notes sobbed like a crying baby.

Once, Annie tried to sing and play the piano for her parents' guests. Her performance made everyone squirm in their chairs. Annie was so embarrassed that she went up to her room and cried. She couldn't play the recorder or the cello. She couldn't play the piano or sing or play the trumpet. Annie had never felt so sad in her life.

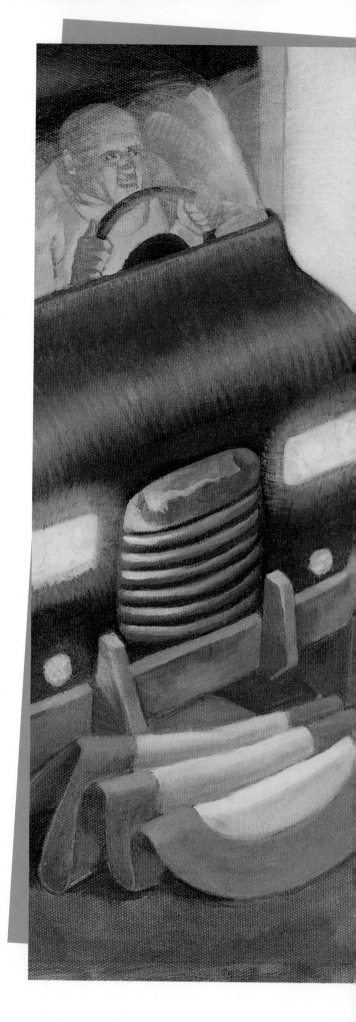

Sometimes, when Annie was sad, she liked to write poetry to make herself feel better. She decided to write a poem about music.

I love to hear music play.
I practice hard every day.
But even though I try and try,
the sounds I play
make people laugh and cry.

That night, Annie put her poem on Daddy's pillow. Then she went to sleep.

In the morning, Daddy and Momma had a long talk with Annie.

"I just can't seem to do anything right," Annie sighed.

"Yes, you can," Daddy said. "There are lots of things you can do."

"Really, Daddy?" Annie asked.

"Of course," Momma said. "Not everyone can play the piano and sing like Patty. Not everyone can play the trumpet like Lee. That's his special gift. And not everyone can write poetry and draw beautiful pictures the way you can."

"I didn't think about it that way," Annie said. "I can't sing or play an instrument well, but I can do *a lot* of other things."

Now, if you should pass by Annie's house, you might hear Patty singing and playing on the piano. Perhaps you'll hear Lee playing his trumpet. And sometimes, if you stop and listen very, very closely, you might hear Annie playing . . .

her radio!

Annie plays loud, finger-popping music when she feels like laughing and drawing pictures. She plays soft, sweet music when she writes her poems. She can play any kind of music she likes on her radio.

She still can't play the piano or sing like Patty, and she still can't play the trumpet like Lee.

But now Annie has found she's happiest when drawing her pictures and writing poetry. Because art and writing are Annie's gifts.

About the Author
Angela Shelf Medearis

Angela Shelf Medearis wrote *Annie's Gifts* for her older sister and younger brother. She based the book on her own childhood. Like Annie, Ms. Medearis discovered early that she had a talent that brought her great joy. Ms. Medearis also loves to read. She especially enjoys reading picture books, which she says are "a child's first step into a lifetime of reading."

About the Illustrator
Anna Rich

Anna Rich discovered her talents as an artist when she was very young. Even in kindergarten, she enjoyed both drawing and coloring.

Remember

by Nikki Grimes

I remember that time
I stood on stage
at the Countee Cullen Library
and recited my poem
and hardly noticed
how loudly my knees
were knocking
'cause you were there
smiling from the front row
to let me know
that I was doing
just fine.

Reader Response

Let's Talk

If you could choose a talent, what would it be?

Let's Think

Why do you think Annie left the poem for her father to read?

Test Prep
Let's Write

What did Annie learn about people's gifts? Write about the lesson she learned.

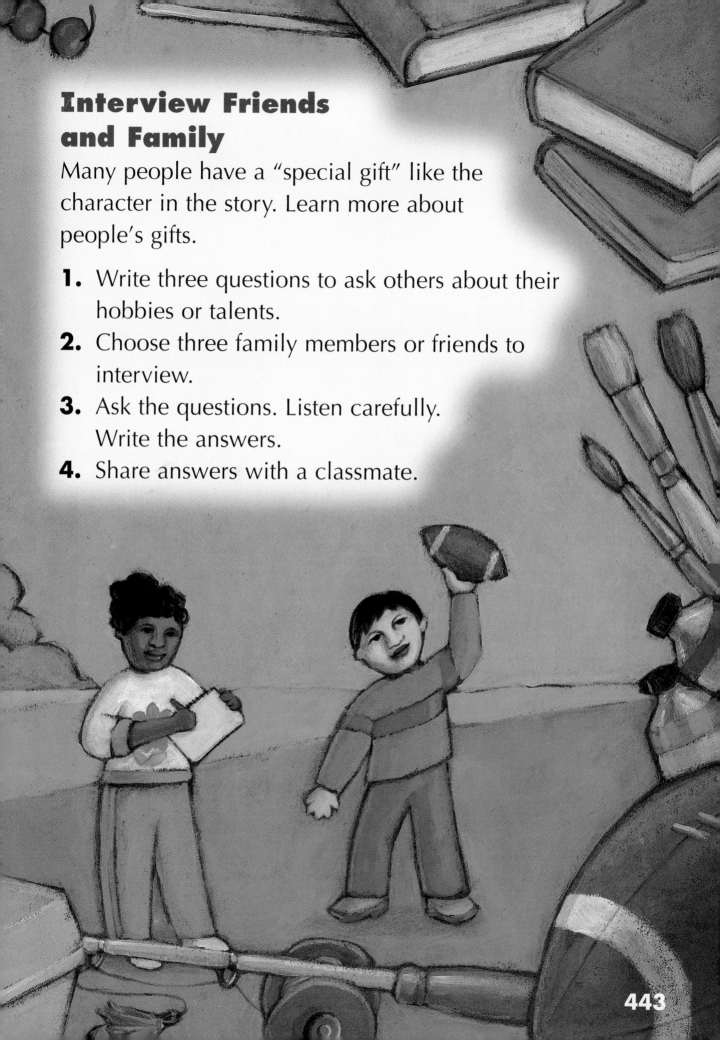

Interview Friends and Family

Many people have a "special gift" like the character in the story. Learn more about people's gifts.

1. Write three questions to ask others about their hobbies or talents.
2. Choose three family members or friends to interview.
3. Ask the questions. Listen carefully. Write the answers.
4. Share answers with a classmate.

Language Arts

More About Commas

Sometimes two sentences are joined together by connecting words such as **and, but,** and **so.** Use a comma before the connecting word.

Mike loves to draw. He loves to paint.
Mike loves to draw**, and** he loves to paint.

Nola cannot paint. She can play the violin.
Nola cannot paint**, but** she can play the violin.

Gary's arm is tired. He will let it rest.
Gary's arm is tired**, so** he will let it rest.

Talk

Make up sentences that have the connecting words **and, but,** and **so.** Tell the sentences to your classmates. Tell where you would put a comma.

Write

Join each pair of sentences with a comma and a connecting word. Write each sentence.

1. Gary played golf. Nola played the violin. (and)
2. Mike liked to paint. He did not like to play golf. (but)
3. The painting was wet. Mike waited for it to dry. (so)

Ask three classmates about their talents. Write sentences using connecting words.

Wicker School Takes Action

by Fay Robinson

illustrated by Jerry Tiritilli

Third Street Bridge before action was taken.

Students Upset By Bridge's Condition

April 29—By the train station in our town, there is a bridge. We've all heard stories about it. It was dark. Stains dripped down the walls. Sour-smelling trash was everywhere. The bridge was in very bad condition.

Earl Stone and his friends from Wicker School discuss the bridge.

Many children from Wicker School used that bridge. "There was nothing nice about it," says Earl Stone, nine years old. "It was probably one of the worst in the nation. We had to do something."

Wicker School students and their teacher, Mrs. Pearl, work on a plan.

Earl and his friends were talking about it early one morning. An art teacher, Mrs. Pearl, heard them. "Our boys and girls were upset," she said. "But they already had a plan to improve the bridge's condition."

Wicker School students meet Mayor Lopez.

Students Take Action

"Earl had information about a mural painted by children in Chicago. Earl thought kids from our school could learn to paint a mural under the bridge," said Mrs. Pearl.

Wicker School took action. First, they asked people to sign a petition. Then they went to the mayor. Mrs. Pearl and her students waited for two hours at city hall. "Nothing was going to stop us," she said.

The children draw their plan.

Mayor Lopez gave the okay. In addition, she asked them not to take action until spring vacation.

With Mrs. Pearl's help, children used markers and a large piece of paper to make their plan. In addition, they used rulers and other tools.

How Students Earned Money

Wicker School students set up collection boxes and sold candy. They earned enough money to buy paint, brushes, and the clean-up supplies for the project.

Children set up collection boxes to raise money.

Wicker School students take action to complete the mural.

By the middle of spring vacation, the young artists had already worked over twenty hours. Nothing could stop them! They scoured the walls, then used blue paint. Piece by piece, the picture took shape.

Now, beneath the bridge is a big painting of our Earth. Children from all nations dance around the Earth in the painting.

Mrs. Pearl and her students enjoy the finished mural.

Students Get an Education

What did the children learn?

"I learned how much work it is to paint something so big," says ten-year-old Eric Miller.

"I feel proud that I helped make our town a little nicer," says Barb Soto.

What is the town's reaction? "They earned something money can't buy," says John Sherry, store owner. "They earned our respect."

It seems there is one lesson everyone learned. By working together, our kids can make a big difference!

City Green

by DyAnne DiSalvo-Ryan

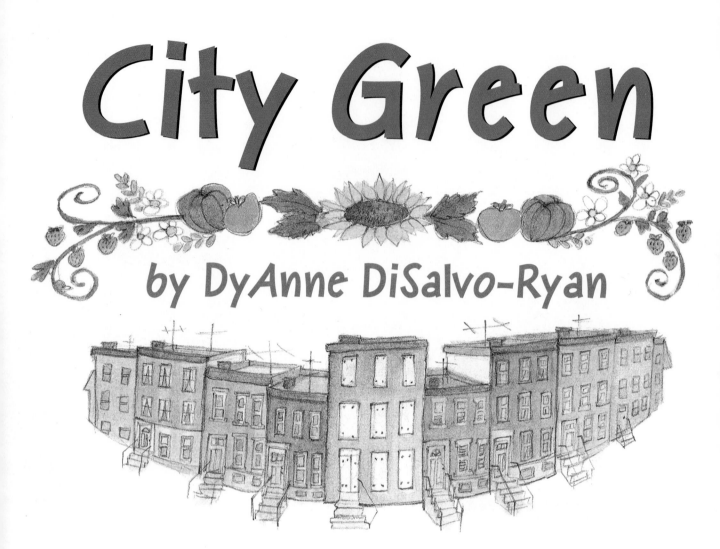

There used to be a building right here on this lot. It was three floors up and down, an empty building nailed up shut for as long as I could remember. My friend Miss Rosa told me Old Man Hammer used to live there—some other neighbors too. But when I asked him about that, he only hollered, "Scram."

Old Man Hammer seems hard as nails.

Last year two people from the city came by, dressed in suits and holding papers. They said, "This building is unsafe. It will have to be torn down."

By winter a crane with a wrecking ball was parked outside. Mama gathered everyone to watch from our front window. In three slow blows that building was knocked into a heap of pieces. Then workers took the rubble away in a truck and filled the hole with dirt.

Now this block looks like a big smile with one tooth missing. Old Man Hammer sits on his stoop and shakes his head. "Look at that piece of junk land on a city block," Old Man Hammer says. "Once that building could've been saved. But nobody even tried."

And every day when I pass this lot it makes me sad to see it.

Then spring comes, and right on schedule Miss
Rosa starts cleaning her coffee cans. Miss Rosa and
I keep coffee cans outside our windowsills. Every
year we buy two packets of seeds at the hardware
store—sometimes marigolds, sometimes zinnias,
and one time we tried tomatoes. We go to the park,
scoop some dirt, and fill up the cans halfway.

This time Old Man Hammer stops us on the way to the park. "This good for nothing lot has plenty of dirt right here," he says.

Then all at once I look at Miss Rosa. And she is smiling back at me. "A *lot* of dirt," Miss Rosa says.

"Like one big coffee can," I say.

That's when we decide to do something about this lot.

Quick as a wink, I'm digging away, already thinking of gardens and flowers. But Old Man Hammer shakes his finger. "You can't dig more dirt than that. This lot is city property."

Miss Rosa and I go to see Mr. Bennett. He used to work for the city. "I seem to remember a program," he says, "that lets people rent empty lots."

That's how Miss Rosa and I form a group of people from our block. We pass around a petition that says: WE WANT TO LEASE THIS LOT. In less than a week we have plenty of names.

"Sign with us?" I ask Old Man Hammer.

"I'm not signing," he says. "Nothing is going to happen."

But something did.

The next week, a bunch of us take a bus to city hall. We walk up the steps to the proper office and hand the woman our list. She checks her files and types some notes and makes some copies. "That will be one dollar, please."

We rent the lot from the city that day. It was just as simple as that.

Saturday morning I'm up with the sun and looking at this lot. My mama looks out too. "Marcy," she says, and hugs me close. "Today I'm helping you and Rosa."

After shopping, Mama empties her grocery bags and folds them flat to carry under her arm. "Come on, Mrs. B.," Mama tells her friend. "We're going to clear this lot."

Then what do you know but my brother comes along. My brother is tall and strong. At first, he scratches his neck and shakes his head just like Old Man Hammer. But Mama smiles and says, "None of that here!" So all day long he piles junk into those bags and carries them to the curb.

Now, this time of day is early. Neighbors pass by and see what we're doing. Most say, "We want to help too." They have a little time to spare. Then this one calls that one and that one calls another.

"Come on and help," I call to Old Man Hammer.

"I'm not helping anybody," he hollers. "You're all wasting your time."

Sour grapes my mama'd say, and sour grapes is right.

Just before supper, when we are good and hungry, my mama looks around this lot. "Marcy," she says, "you're making something happen here."

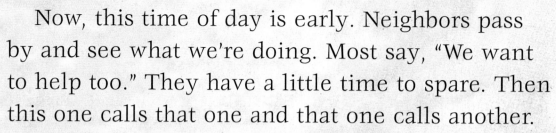

Next day the city drops off tools like rakes and brooms, and a Dumpster for trash. Now there are even more neighbors to help. Miss Rosa, my brother, and I say "Good morning" to Old Man Hammer, but Old Man Hammer just waves like he's swatting a fly.

"Why is Old Man Hammer so mean and cranky these days?" my brother asks.

"Maybe he's really sad," I tell him. "Maybe he misses his building."

"That rotten old building?" My brother shrugs. "He should be happy the city tore down that mess."

"Give him time," Miss Rosa says. "Good things take time."

Mr. Bennett brings wood—old slats he's saved—
and nails in a cup. "I knew all along I saved them
for something," he says. "This wood's good wood."

Then Mr. Rocco from two houses down comes,
carrying two cans of paint. "I'll never use these," he
says. "The color's too bright. But here, this lot could
use some brightening up."

Well, anyone can tell with all the excitement that something is going on. And everyone has an idea about what to plant—strawberries, carrots, lettuce, and more. Tulips and daisies, petunias, and more! Sonny turns the dirt over with a snow shovel. Even Leslie's baby tries to dig with a spoon.

For lunch, Miss Rosa brings milk and jelly and bread and spreads a beach towel where the junk is cleared. By the end of the day a fence is built and painted as bright as the sun.

Later, Mama kisses my cheek and closes my bedroom door. By the streetlights I see Old Man Hammer come down his steps to open the gate and walk into the back of this lot. He bends down quick, sprinkling something from his pocket and covering it over with dirt.

In the morning I tell my brother. "Oh, Marcy," he says. "You're dreaming. You're wishing too hard."

But I know what I saw, and I tell my mama, "Old Man Hammer's planted some seeds."

Right after breakfast, I walk to the back of this lot. And there it is—a tiny raised bed of soil. It is neat and tidy, just like the rows we've planted. Now I know for sure that Old Man Hammer planted something. So I pat the soil for good luck and make a little fence to keep the seeds safe.

Every day I go for a look inside our garden lot. Other neighbors stop in too. One day Mrs. Wells comes by. "This is right where my grandmother's bedroom used to be," she says. "That's why I planted my flowers there."

I feel sad when I hear that. With all the digging and planting and weeding and watering, I'd forgotten about the building that had been on this lot. Old Man Hammer had lived there too. I go to the back, where he planted his seeds. I wonder if this was the place where his room used to be.

I look down. Beside my feet, some tiny stems are sprouting. Old Man Hammer's seeds have grown! I run to his stoop. "Come with me!" I beg, tugging at his hand. "You'll want to see."

I walk him past the hollyhocks, the daisies, the peppers, the rows of lettuce. I show him the strawberries that I planted. When Old Man Hammer sees his little garden bed, his sour grapes turn sweet. "Marcy, child." He shakes his head. "This lot was good for nothing. Now it's nothing but good," he says.

Soon summertime comes, and this lot really grows. It fills with vegetables, herbs, and flowers. And way in the back, taller than anything else, is a beautiful patch of yellow sunflowers. Old Man Hammer comes every day. He sits in the sun, eats his lunch, and sometimes comes back with supper.

Nobody knows how the sunflowers came—not Leslie, my brother, or Miss Rosa. Not Mr. Bennett, or Sonny, or anyone else. But Old Man Hammer just sits there smiling at me. We know whose flowers they are.

About the Author

DyAnne DiSalvo-Ryan

DyAnne DiSalvo-Ryan lives in New York City. She considers the city very important to her work.

"Living in New York City brings my art to life," she says. "When I ride the subways, I sketch the people I see."

Ms. DiSalvo-Ryan remembers clearly the house she lived in as a girl. She loved her Brooklyn neighborhood. Both influenced her work.

Reader Response

Let's Talk

What other things could you do with an empty lot?

Let's Think

Why did Marcy keep Old Man Hammer's secret about the flowers?

Test Prep
Let's Write

Pretend that you are starting a community garden. Write a letter to neighbors and friends asking for their help. Give three reasons why a community garden would be good for your neighborhood.

Make a Mural

Imagine what the garden looks like in the story. Work with friends to make a garden mural. Use it to brighten up your classroom.

1. Look through books about flowers and plants. Find colorful and interesting plants and flowers.
2. Use a large sheet of paper, paint, markers, and colored paper to create the garden.
3. Hang your garden mural on a wall.

Paragraphs

A **paragraph** is a group of sentences about the same idea. The first word starts a few spaces from the left.

My class will plant a garden this spring. Our parents are giving us seeds to plant. The principal said we could plant the garden in front of the school. I can't wait to see the flowers grow!

Look at the first sentence. It tells the main idea. The other sentences tell more about the main idea. When you write a paragraph, make sure your sentences are about the main idea.

Talk

Talk about the picture. What is the main idea? Say it in a sentence. Take turns adding sentences about the main idea.

Write

Write the paragraph. Leave out the sentences that are not about the main idea.

It is easy to plant a flower. First, you need a seed. Then you need to plant the seed in dirt. Sally got dirt on her pants! Finally, you need to water your seed. Water is very good for you. Make sure you put your plant in sunlight.

Write a paragraph about something you have done. Your first sentence should tell the main idea. Your other sentences should tell more about the main idea.

The Clubhouse

Lemonade for Sale

above
few
ice
kept
number
sound

Start Collecting! It's Fun!

The Puddle Pail

castle
crocodile
eight
puddle
road
round
shadows
young

Stone Soup

Stone Soup

add
both
contest
delicious
judges
making
mean
stranger

Wicker School Takes Action

City Green

already
empty
nothing
piece
soil
used

A Good Idea

Annie's Gifts

also
group
radio
squeaked
though
tried

Test Talk

Write Your Answer

Some test questions ask you to write the answer. You will need to look back at the story to find the answer. You must use words from the story to write your answer correctly.

Read these paragraphs and a question about *Annie's Gifts*.

> Annie was so embarrassed that she went up to her room and cried. She couldn't play the recorder or cello. She couldn't play the piano or sing or play the trumpet. Annie had never felt so sad in her life.
> Sometimes, when Annie was sad, she liked to write poetry to make herself feel better. She decided to write a poem about music.

1. What did Annie do to make herself feel better? Write your answer.

What is the question asking? Find the words in the paragraphs to write your answer.

Here is how one boy chose his answer.

I need to find out what Annie does to make herself feel better. One paragraph says that Annie wrote poetry to make herself feel better. I will use those words to write my answer.

Try it!

Use what you learned to answer this question about *Annie's Gifts*. Look at page 436 to find words to write your answer.

2. What are Annie's gifts? Write your answer.

Glossary

Words from Your Stories

a·ble

If you are **able** to do something, you have the power to do it: *Some animals are* **able** *to see well in the dark.*

above

a·bove

The sun is **above** *the hills. Read the line* **above** *the picture.*

add

To **add** is to put numbers or things together: **Add** *5 and 3 to make 8. The cook will* **add** *two more eggs to the batter.*

a·go

Ago means in the past: *I saw him two weeks* **ago**. *Long* **ago** *people lived in caves.*

al·read·y

She ran to the bus stop, but the bus had **already** *gone. He has* **already** *read this book.*

al·so

Tom has a dog, but he likes cats **also**. *Sara likes to ride her bike to school, but she* **also** *likes to walk.*

at·ten·tion

When you give something or someone **attention**, you are giving it thought or care: *Pay* **attention** *while she explains this math problem. The boy gives his dog a lot of* **attention**.

Bb

beach

beach

A **beach** is an area of land found next to a body of water. A **beach** is covered with sand or stones.

behind

be·gan

She **began** *to sing. Snow* **began** *to fall.*

be·hind

He is walking **behind** *her. Her class is* **behind** *in its work.*

both

Both *houses are pink.* **Both** *dogs are mine.*

brook

A **brook** is a small stream of running water. Another word for **brook** is **creek**.

Cc

calm

When someone or something is **calm**, they are quiet or still: *The lake is* **calm** *today. She was frightened, but she answered with a* **calm** *voice. Please* **calm** *down.*

castle

cas·tle

A **castle** is a large building with thick walls and a tower, or something like it: *The king lives in a* **castle**. *We made a sand* **castle**.

cir·cled

When you have **circled** something, you have gone around it in a ring: *The plane* **circled** *the airport until the fog lifted and it was able to land. The spaceship* **circled** *Earth.*

claws

Claws are the sharp, curved nails on the foot of an animal or bird.

con·test

A **contest** is something you enter to win a prize. **Contests** can be between two people or many people: *I entered a cooking* **contest**.

course

A **course** is the direction taken: *After reading the compass, the captain decided to take a* **course** *straight north.*

crea·ture

A **creature** is any living person or animal: *We fed the lost dog because the poor* **creature** *was hungry.*

crocodile

croc·o·dile

A **crocodile** is a large animal with thick skin, four short legs, and a pointed nose. A **crocodile** looks a lot like an alligator.

crops

Crops are plants grown by farmers for food. *Corn and wheat are important* **crops** *in the United States.*

Dd

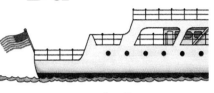

deck

deck

A **deck** is one of the floors of a ship. A **deck** divides a ship into different levels.

de·li·cious

When something is **delicious**, it tastes or smells very good: *The cookies were* **delicious.**

dif·fer·ent

Different means not alike: *Leaves have* **different** *shapes. Basketball is* **different** *from baseball.*

dock

A **dock** is a platform built at the edge of the water. Ships load and unload at a **dock.**

Ee

ear·ly

1 **Early** means near the beginning of something: **Early** *in the school year, the children didn't know each other very well.*
2 **Early** also means before the usual time: *She got up* **early** *yesterday morning.*

Earth

Earth

Earth is the planet we live on. The planet **Earth** moves around the sun.

edge

An **edge** is the line or place where something ends: *We stopped at the **edge** of town.*

eight

Eight is one more than seven; 8.

emp·ty

empty

When something is **empty**, there is nothing inside: *She finished her cereal and left the **empty** bowl. We played in an **empty** lot.*

ev·er

*Is he **ever** at home? When will she **ever** get here?*

fam·i·ly

1 A **family** is a father, mother, and their children. The people who you live with and who take care of you are your **family**.
2 Your **family** is also all of your relatives: *Grandmother invited the **family** for Thanksgiving dinner.*

feath·ers

feathers

Feathers are the light, soft things that cover a bird's body.

few

1 Few means not many: ***Few** people came to the meeting.*
2 A **few** is a small number: *Pick the ripe apples and take a **few** to your grandparents.*

fi·nal·ly

Finally means at last: *Our team finally won a game.*

floating

float·ing

When something or someone is **floating**, they are moving slowly on top of the water or in the air. *The balloon was floating through the air. The jellyfish was floating in the sea.*

flopped

When you have **flopped**, you have dropped or fallen down in a heavy way: *Mother was so tired she flopped into a chair.*

front

1 The **front** is the part of anything that faces forward: *The dog stood on its front feet.*
2 The **front** is also the first part or beginning: *Move to the front of the line.*

 Gg

gathered

gath·ered

When you have **gathered** something, you have collected things or brought things together. When people come together, they have **gathered**: *Tom gathered his tools and went to fix his bike. The crowd gathered to hear the speaker.*

487

giant

gi·ant

When something is **giant**, it is very big:
*I made a **giant** sandwich for lunch and shared
it with my brothers. The dinosaur made **giant**
tracks.* Another word for **giant** is **huge**.

group

1 A **group** is a number of people or things
together: *We saw a **group** of children playing.*
2 To **group** means to gather a number of
people or things together: *I **grouped** the
pictures of all the cats on one page.*

grow

To **grow** is to get bigger: *A cactus will **grow** in
sand. When I **grow** up I want to be a teacher.*

growl

To **growl** is to make a deep or angry sound:
*The dog **growled** at the squirrels. My stomach
is **growling**.*

Hh

head, *def. 1*

head

1 The **head** is the top part of the human
body, or the front part of most animal
bodies. The **head** is where the eyes, ears,
nose, mouth, and brain are.
2 The **head** is also the top or front part of
something: *We put the pillow at the **head** of
the bed. She went to the **head** of the line.*

hel·met

A **helmet** is a covering to protect the head. **Helmets** can be made out of metal, plastic, leather, and other materials.

hos·pi·tal

A **hospital** is a place where sick people are cared for: *Doctors and nurses work in a* **hospital.**

ice

ice

Ice is frozen water: *The pond turns to* **ice** *in winter. I put some* **ice** *in my lemonade.*

im·por·tant

1 When something is **important**, it has great meaning or value: *It is* **important** *that you learn to read well.*
2 When someone is **important**, that person is famous or powerful: *The President is a very* **important** *person in the United States.*

in·ter·est·ing

When something is **interesting**, it holds your attention: *The book was so* **interesting** *that I did not want to stop reading.*

judges

judges

1 **Judges** are people who decide questions of right and wrong under the law.
2 **Judges** also decide the winner of a contest: *The* **judges** *gave Grandma's jam a first-place medal.*

Kk

kitchen

kept

She **kept** *my secret. He has* **kept** *all their letters. I* **kept** *track of our sales.*

kitch·en

A **kitchen** is a room where food is cooked and stored.

Ll

large

large

Large means big: *We live in a* **large** *apartment building.* **Large** *crowds come to see the team play.*

los·es

When someone **loses**, they do not win: *If our team* **loses** *this game, we won't make it to the finals.*

Mm

mak·ing

1 When you are **making** something, you are putting it together or building it: *We are* **making** *soup for dinner.*

2 When you are **making** something, you can also be causing it to happen: *Please stop* **making** *noise.*

3 When you are **making** money, you are getting money for doing something: *We are* **making** *money selling lemonade.* ● **makes, made, mak•ing.**

mean

1 When you **mean** to do something, you have it in mind as a goal or you want to do it: *He didn't* **mean** *to break the glass.*

2 When one thing **means** another, they are the same: *Automobile* **means** *the same thing as car.* ● means, meant, mean•ing.

morn•ing

1 **Morning** is the part of the day between nighttime and noon: *He got up early this* **morning.**

2 **Morning** also means active or experienced at that time of day: *I am a* **morning** *person.*

morning

Nn

near

When something is **near** it is close, or not far away: *We live* **near** *a lake. My birthday is* **near.**

noth•ing

There was **nothing** *in the empty closet.* **Nothing** *could stop the team from winning.*

num•ber

number, *def. 2*

1 A **number** is a word that tells how many. Two is a **number.** Twenty-one is a **number.**

2 A **number** is also a figure or group of figures that stands for a **number.** 9 is a **number.** 21 is a **number.**

3 To **number** is to give a **number** to: *We will* **number** *the boxes as we fill them.*

Oo

oven

ov·en

The **oven** is the part of a stove that you use to bake things in: *The turkey is in the* **oven.**

own

1 When you **own** something, you have it or keep it because you bought it or because someone gave it to you: *I* **own** *a bicycle.*
2 **Own** also means belonging to you: *I make my* **own** *bed every morning.*

Pp

pa·per

1 **Paper** is what you use to write, print, or draw on. **Paper** is also used for wrapping packages and covering walls. Many bags are made of **paper. Paper** is made from wood.
2 A **paper** is also something with writing or printing on it, such as an essay: *Our teacher collected the* **papers** *we had written.*

piece

piece

A **piece** is one of the parts into which something is divided or broken: *I found the last* **piece** *of the puzzle and will now finish it.*

poke

When you **poke** something, you push against it with force: *He* **poked** *me in the side with his elbow.*

present

pres·ent

A **present** is a gift: *His uncle sent him a birthday* **present**.

prob·a·bly

Probably means likely: *You* **probably** *know my brother. We should* **probably** *wait for them.*

pud·dle

A **puddle** is a small amount of water: *The rain left a big* **puddle** *near the steps.*

Rr

radio

ra·di·o

A **radio** is an electric machine that plays voices and music. A **radio** may be small enough to carry in your pocket.

read·y

When you are **ready**, you are all set to do something. When something is **ready** it has been prepared: *Are they* **ready** *to leave for the movie? Lunch is* **ready**.

re·al·ly

1 Really means truly: *Some adventure stories are fun to read, but they could not* **really** *happen.*
2 Really also means very: *I am* **really** *hungry.*

re·mem·ber

When you **remember** something, you call it back to your mind: *I can't* **remember** *their address.*

493

road

road

A **road** is a way to go between places, especially a way for a car, truck, or bus to go along: *This **road** goes to the city.*

rock·ets

Rockets are long metal tubes open at one end. When fuel in the **rockets** is lighted, it burns quickly and drives the rockets forward or straight up. **Rockets** are used to launch spacecraft.

round

Round means shaped like a ball or a circle. The Earth is **round**. A wheel is **round**.

Ss

shadows

se·cret·ly

When something is done **secretly**, it is kept hidden from most people: *We enter our clubhouse **secretly**.*

shad·ows

Shadows are the dark shapes made when something blocks the light.

soil

Soil is the top layer of the ground: *Our garden has such rich **soil** that almost anything will grow in it.* Another word for **soil** is **dirt**.

some·day

Someday means at a future time: ***Someday** we will take a trip to Canada.*

sound

1 A **sound** is something you hear: *He heard the* **sound** *of a dog barking. What is the* **sound** *of the a in* hat?

2 To **sound** is to make a **sound** or **sounds**: *The wind* **sounds** *like a whistle blowing. The words* ate *and* eight **sound** *alike.*

spe·cial

Special means unusual or different in some way: *Your birthday is a* **special** *day.*

squeaked

When something has **squeaked**, it has made a short, sharp, loud sound: *The chair* **squeaked** *when I sat on it.*

steers

steers

When a person **steers** something, he or she is causing it to go in a certain direction. A person who **steers** something is guiding or controlling it: *The little cat* **steers** *the boat.*

still

1 When something is **still,** it is quiet or not moving: *Please keep* **still** *while I am on the telephone.*

2 **Still** also means up to and including now: *Golf is* **still** *a popular game.*

stone

stone

stone

Stone is hard rock: *Over time, the ash turned to* **stone.**

sto·ry

A **story** is words put together that tell about people and places and what happens to them. A **story** can be true or make-believe.

stran·ger

A **stranger** is a person you have not known, seen, or heard of before: *After meeting some other kids, she was no longer a* **stranger.**

sure

When you are **sure,** you are feeling no doubt about something: *Are you* **sure** *you locked the front door?* Another word for **sure** is **certain.**

Tt

team

team

A **team** is a group of people working or playing together: *My sister is on the soccer* **team.**

things

Please put these **things** *away. What kind of* **things** *do you do after school?*

though

Though *it looked like rain, we went on our hike anyway. Even* **though** *I tried, I couldn't do it.*

to·day

Today is this day: **Today** *is my uncle's birthday. Are you going swimming* **today**?

told

She **told** *me about the play. Has she* **told** *you about it?*

trade

A **trade** is getting something in return for giving something: *An apple for an orange at lunch today was a fair* **trade**.

trade

tried

He **tried** *to pick up the chair. She has* **tried** *on several pairs of shoes.*

try

If you **try**, you set out to do something if you can: *Let's* **try** *to cut the grass before noon.*

Uu

up·on

Once **upon** *a time there were three elves. The elves sat* **upon** *the bed.* **Upon** *my word, it's true!*

upon

used

1 When something is **used** it is put into service: *I used a brush on my dog's fur.*

2 **Used** also means not new: *My parents bought a* **used** *car.*

used to means once did: *There* **used to** *be a building on this empty lot.*

Ww

wash, *def. 1*

wash

1 To **wash** is to clean with soap and water: *Be sure to **wash** your hands before dinner. It is his turn to **wash** the dishes.*

2 A **wash** is a bundle of dirty clothes that needs to be washed: *Put your jeans and socks in the **wash**.*

word

1 A **word** is a sound or group of sounds that means something. We speak **words** when we talk.

2 A **word** is also the written or printed letters that stand for a word: *This page is filled with **words** that I can read.*

3 When you give someone your **word**, you give them a promise.

Yy

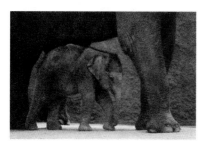

young

years

Years are periods of time: *He's been driving a bus for many* **years.** A **year** has twelve months. The new **year** starts on January 1.

young

When something is **young**, it is in the early part of life. **Young** is the opposite of old: *The* **young** *elephant stood near its mother.*

Writer's Handbook

Contents

Sentences

A **sentence** is a group of words that tells a complete idea.

The **subject** of a sentence tells who or what does something.
The **predicate** of a sentence tells what the subject does.

Subject	Predicate
My aunt	plays tennis in the park.

A **statement** is a sentence that tells something. It begins with a capital letter. It ends with a **.**.

We took a trip on our bikes**.**

A **question** is a sentence that asks something. It begins with a capital letter. It ends with a **?**.

Do you think we can get up this hill**?**

A **command** is a sentence that tells someone to do something. It begins with a capital letter. It ends with a **.**.

Get ready to clean up your desk**.**

An **exclamation** is a sentence that shows surprise or strong feelings. It begins with a capital letter. It ends with an **!**.

Terry won first prize**!**

Nouns

A **noun** is a word that names a person, place, animal, or thing.

The **boy** spent his **vacation** on a **farm**.

Special names for people, places, and animals are called **proper nouns**. Proper nouns begin with capital letters.

Ms. Thomas showed us a video.

A **singular noun** names one person, place, animal, or thing.

The **frog** lives in the **pond**.

A **plural noun** names more than one person, place, animal, or thing. Add **–s** to most nouns to name more than one.

I have two **apples** in my lunch. Sometimes I bring **pears**.

Add **–es** to a noun that ends in **s**, **ch**, **sh**, or **x** to name more than one.

How many school **buses** are there? Mom bought **bunches** of flowers.

As a writer...

I use nouns to give my readers important information.

Some nouns change spelling
to name more than one.

Singular Nouns	Plural Nouns
goose	geese
foot	feet
tooth	teeth
wolf	wolves
leaf	leaves
mouse	mice
knife	knives

A noun that shows who or what owns something
is a **possessive noun.** Add an apostrophe **'** and **–s**
when the noun is singular.

The rabbit was a gift <u>to Sara.</u>
It is **Sara's** rabbit.

Add an apostrophe **'** after **–s** when the noun is plural.

The mother <u>of the boys</u> will be here soon.
The **boys'** mother will be here soon.

Verbs

A **verb** is a word that can show action.

The swimmer **dives** from the board.

Verbs may tell what one person, animal, or thing does. Add **–s** to these verbs.

Maddie **comes** to breakfast at 8:00.

Verbs may tell what more than one person, animal, or thing does. Do not add **–s** to these verbs.

The cars **stop** at the light.

Verbs can tell about action that takes place in the present, in the past, or in the future.

Mom **walks** the dog every day.
Mom **walked** to the store yesterday.
Mom **will walk** with me to school tomorrow.

Some verbs do not show action. The verbs **am, is, are, was,** and **were** do not show action.

Am, is, and are tell about now.	Was and were tell about the past.
I **am** in the second grade. Tom **is** in first grade. We **are** both in the same school.	Alice **was** in first grade last year. We **were** in the same class.

Adjectives

An **adjective** describes a noun. An adjective may tell how many, what size, or what shape.

There are **six** presents in the bag.
They are all in **small** boxes.
They are tied with **thin** ribbons.

An **adjective** describes a noun.
An adjective may tell how something looks, feels, sounds, tastes, or smells.

The **yellow** rose is from Dad.
The **soft** kitten sat in my lap.
The **loud** music came from the TV.
We tried the **salty** nuts.
A **sweet** smell came from the oven.

Use adjectives when you compare nouns. Add **–er** to an adjective when you compare two nouns. Add **–est** when you compare more than two nouns.

Paula is **tall**.
Tom is **taller** than Paula.
Bill is **tallest** of all.

Adverbs

An **adverb** is a word that tells about a verb. Use an adverb to tell when, where, or how an action takes place.

Our class will go to the museum **tomorrow**. Mom and I go **there** every Saturday. We talk **softly** in the library.

Pronouns

A **pronoun** is a word that takes the place of a noun or nouns. **I**, **he**, **she**, **it**, **we**, and **they** are pronouns.

Alexa rode her bicycle.
She rode her bicycle.

The day was cloudy.
It was cloudy.

Use the pronoun **I** in place of your name.

I like to play the piano.

Pronouns that tell about one person or thing are singular.

The store had many things to sell.
It had many things to sell.

Pronouns that tell about more than one person or thing are **plural**.

 The computers are for our class.
They are for our class.

As a writer...

I use pronouns to take the place of nouns when the meaning is clear.

Singular Pronouns	Plural Pronouns
I	we
you	you
he, she, it	they

Pronouns Before and After Verbs

Some pronouns are the subject of a sentence. They come before the verb. These pronouns are **I, he, she, we, they.**

The pilot is going to Atlanta.
She is going to Atlanta.

Some pronouns come after a verb. These pronouns are **me, him, her, us, them.**

The teacher gave **Sam** a prize.
The teacher gave **him** a prize.

You can use the pronouns **you** and **it** before or after a verb.

It is on the table.
I saw **it** on the table.

Contractions

A **contraction** is a short way to put two words together.
An apostrophe ' takes the place of one or more letters.

My boots **are not** muddy.
My boots **aren't** muddy.

I will come to your house after school.
I'll come to your house after school.

Commas

Use commas to separate three or more words in a list.
I need paper, brushes, and paint for my art class.

Use a comma between the day of the week, the date, and the year.
Our hockey game is on Tuesday, May 18, 200 _.

Use a comma after the greeting and closing in a letter.
Dear Aunt Sara,

> **Love,**
> **Trish**

Sometimes two sentences are joined together by connecting words such as **and, but**, and **so**. Use a comma before the connecting word.

Tom wears gloves, and he also wears a hat.
Erin has a cat, but she also wants a dog.
My mom has a toothache, so she will go to the dentist.

Quotation Marks

Quotation marks " " show the beginning and end of what someone says.

The librarian asked, "Who would like to check out books today?"

"We would," said Juan and Angela.

Paragraphs

A **paragraph** is a group of sentences about the same idea. The first word starts a few spaces from the left. The first sentence in the paragraph often tells the main idea. The other sentences tell more about the main idea.

As a writer...

I check that my sentences make sense when I proofread my work.

Our class is putting on a play. The name of the play is *Goldilocks and the Three Bears.* One person is the narrator. Four are actors. Others are making the set and the costumes. We will invite other classes. We also will invite our families.

Writing a Thank-You Letter

A thank-you letter has the same five parts as a friendly letter. They are the **date**, **greeting**, **body**, **closing**, and **signature**. A comma goes between the date and the year. A comma is also used after the greeting and closing.

In a thank-you letter, the body of the letter thanks someone for something.

Date

October 17, 200_

Greeting

Dear Grandma and Grandpa,

Body

Thank you for the pictures you sent. I am happy to see pictures of you when you were my age. Now, I can see why everyone in the family says I have your eyes, Grandpa, and your smile, Grandma. I have a picture of Mom when she was my age, and I can see how we all look a lot like each other. I will send you some pictures soon. Let me know who you think little brother Timmy looks like.

Closing
Signature

Love,

Kim

Addressing an Envelope

An envelope has two addresses. The **return address** tells who is sending the letter. The **mailing address** tells who will receive the letter. Use a comma between the city and state. Don't forget the zip code!

Return address

Kim Vasquez
543 Downhill Drive
Tucson, Arizona 85726

Mailing address

Mr. and Mrs. Frank Salidas
700 Franklin St.
Encino, California 91416

Sharing a Book

Writing a **book report** is one way to share a book.
Here are some other ways to share.

- **Be a Reporter**
  Be a TV or radio reporter. Make a cardboard frame
  that looks like a TV set or a cardboard microphone
  for a radio report. Tell about a favorite book. You
  might tape-record your show.

- **Fly a Book Kite**
  Make a paper kite. Write the title and author of
  your book. Draw pictures about the book and write
  some interesting words from the book on a long
  paper tail. Hang the kite in your classroom.

- **Advertise on a Poster**
  Make a poster to advertise your book. Draw pictures
  and write some things about your book. Make your
  poster so interesting that your classmates will want
  to read your book.

- **Act It Out**
  Form a group with others who have read the same
  book. Make masks of the main characters.
  Take parts and act out one part or all of the book.

Spelling Lists

Unit 4 The Great Ball Game

1. **bravely** — She **bravely** stepped to the front of the class.
2. **lightly** — The wind blew **lightly** through the trees.
3. **softly** — The baby breathed **softly** as he slept.
4. **friendly** — The coach was very **friendly**.
5. **slowly** — Time passed **slowly** during the test.
6. **weekly** — We have a **weekly** spelling test.
7. **cheer** — The crowd let out a **cheer** when we won.
8. **clear** — It was a **clear** and cool day for the game.
9. **ago** — Dinosaurs lived a long time **ago**.
10. **head** — My neck holds up my **head**.

Birthday Joy
The Best Older Sister

1. **boil** — **Boil** the water to cook the egg.
2. **point** — It is impolite to **point** at someone.
3. **voice** — Your **voice** has a nice sound to it.
4. **coin** — A dime is a **coin**.
5. **spoil** — Don't **spoil** your dinner by eating candy.
6. **enjoy** — I hope you will **enjoy** the show.
7. **colorful** — A Chinese dragon is very **colorful**.
8. **wonderful** — Watching the parade was **wonderful**.
9. **father** — My **father** takes care of me.
10. **told** — I **told** a very good story.

Treasure Pie
Bruno the Baker

1. **bread** — I put peanut butter on **bread**.
2. **spread** — I **spread** jam on the toast.
3. **thread** — Mom used a needle and **thread** to fix the hole.
4. **breath** — My **breath** turned to steam in the cold.
5. **sweat** — Running fast can make you **sweat**.
6. **weather** — The **weather** went from sunny to rainy.
7. **eraser** — An **eraser** can take away wrong answers.
8. **helper** — The classroom **helper** passed out papers.
9. **ready** — I was **ready** to go to the park.
10. **today** — **Today** is my birthday.

Spelling Lists

The Rooster Who Went to His Uncle's Wedding

1.	**climb**	Some bears can **climb** trees.
2.	**lamb**	A **lamb** is a baby sheep.
3.	**knit**	You **knit** with two needles and yarn.
4.	**comb**	**Comb** your hair to make it look nice.
5.	**kneel**	You have to **kneel** to see the worm.
6.	**knot**	I have a **knot** in my shoestring.
7.	**chalk**	The teacher could not find **chalk** to write with.
8.	**sauce**	Tomato **sauce** tastes good on noodles.
9.	**story**	Our teacher read a **story** to us.
10.	**able**	I was **able** to jump over the puddle.

Yawning Dawn
Missing: One Stuffed Rabbit

1.	**awful**	That new movie was **awful**.
2.	**claw**	A cat's **claw** is sharp.
3.	**saw**	I **saw** a good play.
4.	**bought**	Dad and Mom **bought** a new car.
5.	**draw**	My brother can **draw** great pictures.
6.	**straw**	The horse's stall had **straw** in it.
7.	**whoever**	**Whoever** wrote the book knows a lot.
8.	**wrong**	It was **wrong** to break my toy.
9.	**really**	It rained **really** hard last night.
10.	**finally**	I **finally** finished the book.

Space Dreams
Unit 5 Man on the Moon

1.	**camera**	I took those pictures with my **camera**.
2.	**carry**	This bag is too heavy to **carry**.
3.	**lesson**	I learned a good **lesson** about friendship.
4.	**suddenly**	**Suddenly** the lights went off.
5.	**follow**	I will **follow** you to the library.
6.	**pretty**	That sunset is **pretty**.
7.	**cousin**	My **cousin** came to visit.
8.	**double**	Two best friends are **double** the fun.
9.	**began**	The movie **began** at two o'clock.
10.	**ever**	It ended happily **ever** after.

Spelling Lists

Two Lunches at the Mill
Going to Town

1.	**blouse**	I tucked my **blouse** into my pants.
2.	**place**	We can buy hamburgers in this **place**.
3.	**race**	We'll have a **race** in the park.
4.	**blouses**	Mom bought two **blouses** for me.
5.	**places**	Dad has been to many **places**.
6.	**races**	John runs in many **races**.
7.	**people**	There weren't many **people** at the show.
8.	**apple**	I had an **apple** in my lunch.
9.	**only**	I **only** had one cookie.
10.	**word**	I do not know this spelling **word**.

A True Boating Family
Riding the Ferry with Captain Cruz

1.	**after**	Does ten come **after** nine?
2.	**flower**	I picked a **flower** for you.
3.	**sister**	My **sister** has her own room.
4.	**brother**	My **brother** likes to play chess.
5.	**over**	Can you come **over** to my house?
6.	**summer**	I can't wait for the warm days of **summer**.
7.	**statue**	Our town has a **statue** of George Washington.
8.	**glue**	This **glue** is very sticky.
9.	**years**	I've had this book for many **years**.
10.	**which**	**Which** coat is yours?

Splash!
Down in the Sea: The Jellyfish

1.	**neighbor**	My **neighbor** has two dogs.
2.	**sleigh**	You would use a **sleigh** on the snow.
3.	**weigh**	How many pounds do you **weigh**?
4.	**weight**	My **weight** went up last year.
5.	**reindeer**	**Reindeer** live where it is cold.
6.	**veil**	A **veil** covered her face.
7.	**really**	I **really** don't know how it happened.
8.	**mostly**	The Earth is **mostly** made up of water.
9.	**grow**	Mom likes to **grow** vegetables.
10.	**near**	We live **near** a pond.

515

Spelling Lists

Tex and the Big, Bad T. Rex
Let's Go Dinosaur Tracking!

1. **undo**   Can you **undo** this knot?
2. **unhappy**   Are you **unhappy** about the rain?
3. **unlucky**   The **unlucky** girl fell in the mud puddle.
4. **unfair**   It is **unfair** to cheat.
5. **unlike**   The story was **unlike** any other I have read.
6. **untie**   Can you **untie** the ribbon?
7. **expert**   The track star is an **expert** runner.
8. **index**   An **index** is at the back of a book.
9. **front**   Stand at the **front** of the classroom.
10. **probably**   It will **probably** be sunny tomorrow.

The Clubhouse
Unit 6 Lemonade for Sale

1. **calf**   The **calf** followed the cow.
2. **half**   One is **half** of two.
3. **phone**   The **phone** is ringing.
4. **laugh**   I like to **laugh** at cartoons.
5. **rough**   A cat's tongue is **rough**.
6. **tough**   A horse's hide is **tough**.
7. **money**   We use **money** to buy things.
8. **cookie**   I'll share my **cookie** with you.
9. **sound**   The cat did not make a **sound**.
10. **kept**   I **kept** the door open for you.

Start Collecting! It's Fun!
The Puddle Pail

1. **calves**   The cow had two **calves**.
2. **halves**   Two **halves** make a whole.
3. **shelves**   The man put the bread on **shelves**.
4. **wolves**   **Wolves** once roamed the United States.
5. **lives**   Some say a cat has nine **lives**.
6. **leaves**   **Leaves** fall in autumn.
7. **ceiling**   The bug flew to the **ceiling**.
8. **neither**   **Neither** of us could reach it.
9. **road**   A car came down the **road**.
10. **young**   I was afraid of the dark when I was **young**.

516

Stone Soup: A Folktale
Stone Soup

1. **airplane** The **airplane** soared overhead.
2. **chair** Sit on this **chair**.
3. **pair** I have a **pair** of new shoes.
4. **hair** Please comb and brush your **hair**.
5. **care** I took **care** of my little brother.
6. **share** I will **share** my bread with the ducks.
7. **judge** A **judge** will hear the case.
8. **badge** An officer wears a **badge**.
9. **making** We are **making** a cake.
10. **mean** Do you **mean** what you say?

A Good Idea
Annie's Gifts

1. **ache** I have an **ache** in my head.
2. **chorus** We sang in the school **chorus**.
3. **stomach** Your **stomach** helps digest food.
4. **chord** He hit the wrong **chord** on the violin.
5. **echo** An **echo** is a sound coming back to you.
6. **school** We go to **school** to learn.
7. **uniform** Some people wear a **uniform** to work.
8. **music** I hear **music** coming from the computer.
9. **though** I smiled even **though** I was sad.
10. **group** A large **group** of children sat on the grass.

Wicker School Takes Action
City Green

1. **earn** Mom works to **earn** money.
2. **learn** We **learn** important things in school.
3. **heard** I **heard** a woodpecker pecking at a tree.
4. **hour** Noon is the **hour** we eat lunch.
5. **flour** Biscuits are made from **flour**.
6. **sour** Lemons taste **sour**.
7. **action** You should take **action** to help.
8. **section** Which **section** of the newspaper do you want?
9. **piece** I would like a **piece** of pie.
10. **already** Is it time to go **already**?

Tested
Words List

Unit 4

Hear the Cheers

The Great Ball Game

ago
creature
head
loses
still
team

Birthday Joy

The Best Older Sister

attention
different
important
interesting
secretly
special
told

Treasure Pie

Bruno the Baker

kitchen
large
oven
present
ready
today
wash

Paul Goes to the Ball

The Rooster Who Went to His Uncle's Wedding

able
brook
early
feathers
growl
own
story

Yawning Dawn

Missing: One Stuffed Rabbit

calm
family
finally
gathered
hospital
morning
paper
really

Unit 5

Space Dreams

Man on the Moon

began
circled
Earth
ever
remember
rockets
try

Two Lunches at the Mill

Going to Town

behind
crops
edge
sure
trade
upon
word

A True Boating Family

Riding the Ferry with Captain Cruz

course
deck
dock
steers
things
years

Splash!

Down in the Sea: The Jellyfish

beach
floating
flopped
grow
near
poke

Tex and the Big Bad T. Rex

Let's Go Dinosaur Tracking!

claws
front
giant
helmet
probably
someday
stone

Unit 6

The Clubhouse

Lemonade for Sale

above
few
ice
kept
number
sound

Start Collecting! It's Fun!

The Puddle Pail

castle
crocodile
eight
puddle
road
round
shadows
young

Stone Soup: A Folktale

Stone Soup

add
both
contest
delicious
judges
making
mean
stranger

A Good Idea

Annie's Gifts

also
group
radio
squeaked
through
tried

Wicker School Takes Action

City Green

already
empty
nothing
piece
soil
used

Acknowledgments

Text

Page 18: From *Great Ball Game* by Joseph Bruchac, illustated by Susan Roth. Text Copyright © Joseph Bruchac, 1994. Illustrations Copyright © Susan L. Roth, 1994. Published by arrangement with Dial Books For Young Readers, a division of Penguin Putnam Inc.

Page 48: From *The Best Older Sister* by Sook Nyul Choi; ill. by Cornelius Van Wright & Ying-Hwa Hu, copyright © 1997 by Sook Nyul Choi. Illustrations copyright © 1997 by Cornelius Van Wright and Ying-Hwa Hu. Used by permission of Random House Children's Books, a division of Random House, Inc.

Page 67: "Seeing a New Sister" from *Feelings, Lines, Colors* by E. Alma Flagg. Reprinted by permission.

Page 78: *Bruno the Baker* by Lars Klinting. Copyright © 1997 by Lars Klinting. Translation copyright © 1997 by Henry Holt and Company, Inc. Reprinted by permission of Henry Holt and Company Inc. and Groundwood/Douglas & Mc Intyre Children's Books, Canada

Page 112: *The Rooster Who Went to His Uncle's Wedding* by Alma Flor Ada. Copyright © 1993 by Alma Flor Ada. Reprinted by permission of G. P. Putnam's Sons, a division of Penguin Putnam Inc.

Page 144: *Missing: One Stuffed Rabbit* by Maryann Cocca-Leffler. Text and illustrations copyright © 1998 by Maryann Cocca-Leffler. Reprinted by permission of Albert Whitman & Company.

Page 171: "Rosie" from *Lunch Money* by Carol Diggory Shields. Copyright © 1995 by Carol Diggory Shields. Reprinted by permission of Dutton Children's Books, a division of Penguin Putnam Inc.

Page 188: *Man on the Moon* by Anastasia Suen. Illustrated by Benrei Huang. Text Copyright © Anastasia Suen, 1997. Illustration Copyright © Benrei Huang, 1997. Published by arrangement with Viking Children's Books, a division of Penguin Putnam Inc.

Page 216: *Going to Town.* Text adapted from *Little House in the Big Woods* by Laura Ingalls Wilder. Illustrated by Renée Graef. Text copyright © 1932 Laura Ingalls Wilder, renewed © 1959 by Roger Lea MacBride. "Little House" ® is a registered trademark of HarperCollins Publishers, Inc. Illustrations copyright © 1995 by Renée Graef. Reprinted by permission of HarperCollins Publishers.

Page 240: *A True Boating Family* © 1998 David McPhail.

Page 246: *Riding the Ferry with Captain Cruz* by Alice K. Flanagan. Text copyright © 1996 Childrens Press, Inc., a Division of Grolier Publishing Co., Inc. All rights reserved. Reprinted by permission.

Page 257: "Barcarola"/"The Boatman's Song" by Nicolás Guillén from *Por El Mar De Las Antillas Anda Un Barco De Papel,* Lóguez Ediciones. Ctra de Madrid, 90.

Page 268: *Down in the Sea: The Jellyfish* by Patricia Kite. Text copyright © 1993 by L. Patricia Kite. Reprinted by permission of Albert Whitman & Company.

Page 296: From *Let's Go Dinosaur Tracking!* by Miriam Schlein. Copyright © 1991 by Miriam Schlein. Reprinted by permission of the author.

Page 313: "Strange Footprints" by Vivian Gouled. Reprinted by permission.

Page 330: *Lemonade for Sale* by Stuart J. Murphy. Text copyright © 1998 by Stuart Murphy. Illustrations copyright © Tricia Tusa. MathStart ™ is a Trademark of HarperCollins Publishers, Inc. Reprinted by permission.

Page 355: "Lemonade for Sale" from *Mummy Took Cooking Lessons* by John Ciardi. Text copyright © 1990 by Judith C. Ciardi. Illustrations copyright © 1990 by Houghton Mifflin

Company. Reprinted by permission.

Page 366: *The Puddle Pail* by Elisa Kleven. Copyright © 1997 by Elisa Kleven. Reprinted by permission of Dutton Children's Books, a division of Penguin Putnam Inc.

Page 398: "Stone Soup" from *Kid City Magazine*, November 1994. Copyright 1994 Children's Television Workshop (New York, New York). All rights reserved.

Page 409: "Spaghetti! Spaghetti!" from *Rainy Rainy Saturday* by Jack Prelutsky. Text copyright © 1980 by Jack Prelutsky. Used by permission of HarperCollins Publishers.

Page 420: *Annie's Gifts* by Angela Shelf Medearis. Text copyright © 1994 by Angela Shelf Medearis. Illustrations copyright © 1994 by Anna Rich. All rights reserved. Reprinted by permission of Just Us Books Inc.

Page 441: "Remember" from *It's Raining Laughter* by Nikki Grimes. Text copyright © 1997 by Nikki Grimes. Reprinted by permission.

Page 452: *City Green* by DyAnne DiSalvo-Ryan. Copyright © 1994 by DyAnne DiSalvo-Ryan. Used by permission of HarperCollins Publishers.

Selected text and images in this book are copyrighted © 2002.

Artists

Cover illustration © John Sandford
Jeff Philbach, TOC
Jerry Tiritilli, 10, 446–451
Kelly Hume, 12, 216b
Susan L. Roth, 18a, 19–36
Pamela Paulsrud, 18b–c, 38, 48b–c, 56b, 62b, 66b, 456b
Anthony Lewis, 38–41
Anne Sibley O' Brien, 42–47
Yoshi Miyake, 4, 48a, 50–56a, 57–62a, 63–65, 513
Janet Ocwieja, 66a, 170, 235
Lindy Burnett, 67, 258–261
David Austin Clar, 68–71
Susan Swan, 72–77
Lars Klinting, 78–99
Doug Knutson, 101
Anthony Carnabuci, 104, 313
Carolyn Croll, 106–111
Kathleen Kuchera, 112–132
Kathi Ember, 136–139, 176
Helen Lester, 138–143
Maryann Cocca-Leffler, 144–169
Cecily Lang, 145
Laura Ovresat, 174–177, 386–389, 441
Phil Wilson, 178, 310–313, 318
John Sandford, 180
Larry Johnson, 182–189
Benrei Huang, 188–203
Brad Teare, 205, 483b, 486a, 489a, 492a
Margeaux Lucas, 206–209, 355
Miles Hyman, 210–215
Renée Graef, 216–234
Gail Piazza, 236–239
David McPhail, 6, 240–245,495, 514–515
John Zielinski, 246, 254, 257b, c
Shelly Hehenberger, 257a
Allan Eitzen, 262–267
Valerie A. Kells, 283
Roberta Polfus, 285
Reggie Holladay, 286–289
Bernard Adnet, 290–295
Phil Wilson, 296–312, 488a
David Wenzel, 322a

Eliza Schulte Holliday, 322b
Rosario Valderrama, 324–329
Tricia Tusa, 330a, b, 331–353
Bradley Clark, 354c
Cary Pillo, 354
Michael Reid, 356–359
Elisa Kleven, 366–384
Lilly Toy Hong, 390–397
Eileen Mueller Neill, 8, 398–408, 516–517
Nancy Freeman, 409
Toby Williams, 410–413
Nita Winter, 414–419
Anna Rich, 420a, 421–439, 478
Robin Moro, 442–445
DyAnne DiSalvo-Ryan, 452–473
Paul Meisel, 474–477
Kevin O' Malley, 482, 489a, 492a, 497a
Mike Dammer, 483a, 489b, 492b, 498a
Benton Mahan, 487b, 490b, 493b
Randy Chewning, 488b, 491b, 494b

Photographs

Every effort has been made to secure permission and provide
appropriate credit for photographic material. The publisher
deeply regrets any omission and pledges to correct errors
called to their attention in subsequent editions.

Unless otherwise acknowledged, all photographs are the
property of Scott Foresman, a division of Pearson Education.
Page abbreviations are as follows: (t) top, (b) bottom, (l) left, (r)
right, (ins) inset, (s) spot, (bk) background.

Page 12 (C) Corbis Stock Market
Page 13 (C) Corbis Stock Market
Page 14 (T) SuperStock, Inc.
Page 15 (C) Corbis Stock Market
Page 16 (T) The Granger Collection, New York
Page 17 (T) Stock Boston
Page 37 (TL) Courtesy, Greenfield Review Press
Page 66 (C) Courtesy Sook Nyul Choi
Page 100 (TR) Courtesy, Alfabeta Bokforlag Publishers
Page 133 (TC) Courtesy Alma Flor Ada
Page 170 (BL) Richard Hutchings for Scott Foresman
Page 171 (C) E. LeMoine/Jacana/Photo Researchers, Inc.
Page 205 (TR) Courtesy Anastasia Suen
Page 207 (TR) NASA
Page 235 (R) Leslie A. Kelly
Pages 246–255 Christine Osinski

Page 256 Mr. Flanagan
Page 259 (BC) SuperStock; (BC) David Young-Wolff/ PhotoEdit;
(BC) Spencer Grant/Stock Boston; (BC) Chuck Savage/The
Stock Market: (BC) José L. Pelaez Inc./ The Stock Market
Page 268 (C) Randy Morse/TOM STACK & ASSOCIATES
Pages 269–270 Herb Segars
Page 271 (C) Fred Bavendam/Minden Pictures
Page 272 (C) © (date) F. Stuart Westmorland
Page 273 (TL) Neil G. McDaniel
Page 273 (TR) John Lidington/Photo Researchers, Inc.; (CL)
Dave B. Fleetham/TOM STACK & ASSOCIATES; (CR) Herb
Segars
Page 274 Bill Curtsinger; (CR) Sea Studios
Page 275 (TC) David Hall
Page 276 (C) Herb Segars
Page 277 (TC) Bill Curtsinger
Page 278 Sea Studios
Page 279 © (date) F. Stuart Westmorland
Page 280 (CL) TOM STACK & ASSOCIATES; (TR) Carl Roessler;
(CR) Sea Studios
Page 281 (C) Animals Animals/Earth Scenes
Page 282 (C) Animals Animals/Earth Scenes
Page 283 Herb Segars
Page 284 (T) Photo Researchers, Inc.
Page 285 (BL) Gerry Mooney for Scott Foresman
Page 312 (TL) Courtesy Miriam Schlein; (CR) Courtesy Phil
Wilson
Page 354 (TR) Courtesy, HarperCollins Publishers
Page 385 (BC) Courtesy Elisa Kleven
Page 414 (T) Stone
Pages 414–419 Norbert Wu/Tony Stone Images
Page 440 (TL) Courtesy Angela Shelf Medearis; (TR) Artville;
(CL) Courtesy Anna Rich; (B) Artville
Page 473 (BC) Animals Animals/Earth Scenes; (TL) Paul
Sirochman Photography
Page 484 (TL) SuperStock
Page 485 (BL) NASA
Page 486 (BL) /Animals Animals/Earth Scenes
Page 487 (TL) Fred Bavendam/Minden Pictures
Page 496 (BL) Corbis/Stock Market
Page 498 (BL) Animals Animals/Earth Scenes

Glossary

The contents of the glossary have been adapted from the *Scott
Foresman First Dictionary*, Copyright © 2000, Scott Foresman,
a division of Addison Wesley Educational Publishers, Inc.